PRAISE FOR

NEVER TOO LATE

"A vivid, engaging, and heart-warming tribute to that rare and wonderful thing: a late-in-life love."

—**SUSAN WITTIG ALBERT, PH.D**, author of *Loving Eleanor* and *The General's Women* and founder of Story Circle Network

"Do you like romance? Two people young in heart meet through Craigslist, date, wrestle through the challenges of learning about each other—sex, religion, money, health, you name it—and (spoiler alert) get married. For him, a third marriage; for her, a first—at 62. The joy of this book is its honesty. The open conversations. The moments of doubt. The truth of two people who discover each other, care about each other, and live full lives, no matter what the challenges. A book filled with grace and charm."

—**ALINE SOULES**, author of *Meditation on Woman* and her chapbook, *Evening Sun*

"For those who think life has passed them by, take heart, and read B. Lynn Goodwin's book, *Never Too Late*, an unflinchingly honest, personal tale of love found after 60. We discover, along with Goodwin, that the fragile bloom of late life love can flower into a sturdy fullness: of family, shared wisdom, patient understanding, and mutual acceptance. From that first date's knock on the door to trips back home to Tex[illegible] to experience with her a deferred dre[illegible]

—**KATE FARR**[illegible] [illegible]rd-winning antholog[illegible] [illegible]*ng: Women Remembe*[illegible] *70s* and *Cry of the Nightbird: Writers Against Domestic Violence*

"*Never Too Late* is a pleasant, well-written chronicle of an older woman's search for true love—very different from any love story you have ever read."

—**RICHARD J. SMITH**, Ph.D., author of *Life After Eighty, Once Upon A Christmas,* and *Musings of an Old Man*

"At some point in our lives we have all come face to face with the realization that love is not the stuff of Hollywood and cheap fiction, but far more complex, demanding and difficult to navigate regardless of what some may tell us. It is also exhilarating, unfathomable, and beyond our human comprehension. B. Lynn Goodwin gives us a glimpse of both these truths in *Never Too Late.* With refreshing—even, at times, painful candor, Lynn takes us along on her personal journey to discover what it means to give yourself to another person and to learn to accept them just as they are—the way God loves us all. Lynn is an inspiration to those who have ever considered giving up, and at one time or another most of us have. By seizing happiness with courage, sincerity and perseverance Lynn shows us that real love is not superficial, but about living each day as if it the beginning of something wonderful."

—**DOUGLAS A. WEISS**, author of *Life, Love and Internet Dating*

"Few relationships are as complex and multi-layered as the romantic pairing of a man and a woman. And, adding to the potential for miscommunication and conflict, consider the predicament of a 60-year-old, decidedly independent virgin who suddenly finds herself actively wooed by a dynamic, take-charge, traditionally religious man.

"*Never Too Late: From Wannabe To Wife At 62* is the story of B. Lynn Goodwin and her now husband as they progressed along their rocky journey from first tentative kiss to the altar. With candor, humor and an engaging writing style that is sure to keep you turning pages, Lynn delivers a movingly honest account of the various issues, challenges and unexpected delights inherent to building a later-life relationship.

“Boomer women especially will relate to Lynn’s struggle as she shifts between viewing herself as a strong, single woman and the need for making multiple compromises that being part of a couple entails. From railing against old guard established gender roles, to concerns over sharing financial resources, to yearning to feel the warmth of a man’s protective arms, Lynn freely expresses the fluctuating emotions she experienced. Any battle scarred veteran of the Women’s Movement and its gender wars can’t help but understand.

“Whether you have been in a long-standing relationship, are reentering the dating scene or are currently single, if you are a woman of maturity, you are going to relate to Lynn’s story. *Never Too Late* is an honest, insightful look at one of life’s greatest mysteries: the ever changing and ever challenging relationship between a man and a woman. This book is one you won’t want to miss!”

—**MARY EILEEN WILLIAMS**, Host of Feisty Side of Fifty, author of *Land the Job You Love!: 10 Surefire Strategies for Jobseekers Over 50*

Never Too Late:
From Wannabe to Wife at 62

by B. Lynn Goodwin

ISBN 978-1-63393-608-9

Published by

köehlerbooks™

210 60th Street
Virginia Beach, VA 23451
800-435-4811
www.koehlerbooks.com

B. Lynn Goodwin

NEVER TOO LATE

FROM WANNABE TO WIFE AT 62

Best wishes,
B. Lynn Goodwin-Brown
12/09/19

VIRGINIA BEACH
CAPE CHARLES

PROLOGUE

LATE THURSDAY AFTERNOON. My mind whirled. Staring at a TV rerun did not calm me.

What if I tripped? Or said something rude? Or sounded like an idiot? What if my good pants didn't go around me anymore? Or if my black top with the low, square neck squeezed against my oversized breasts, pushing them up and showing too much?

It's a date, not your last date, I thought as I reached for the remote. Now get up and get ready.

In my bedroom, I pulled on my tan, silk pants. The elastic bit into my waist. My black shirt did nothing to hide my muffin top. It'd been forty years since I was first told, *if you want to get a boyfriend, lose weight.*

Not going back there. Ever!

Richard saw my picture before he asked me out. Hopefully, my weight wouldn't bother him. Besides, a man's eyes were likely to be focused about eight inches higher.

I looked into the mirror, removed my glasses, and squinted. My eyebrows were wispy as a newborn's hair. That wouldn't do. Gently darkening them with brown liner, I hoped that they would not look drawn on. It wasn't enough. Two softly smudged shadows gave my eyelids depth. Then I pulled out the plum lipstick I purchased six years earlier. Still moist enough.

Picking up my black Naot shoes with tan curlicues, my confidence grew. They would support my arches and give me a better chance of walking smoothly. Two weeks earlier, I went right, Mikko McPuppers went left, and we collided instead of avoiding each other. Struggling to stay on my feet, I crashed into the wall. My right shoulder, hip, knee, and anklebone screamed out. Or maybe the scream came from my mouth. I hurt too much to know the difference. As I hobbled into the dining room, Mikko followed me with his head lowered. Gazing up at me, his eyes said, "Sorry, person. Can I get you an ice pack?"

"It's not your fault, little one. Really. I'll be okay."

Tonight, thankfully, adrenaline overrode my pain just as it overrode my fear when I gave Richard the best times to call. My fingers shook as I fastened the strap on my left shoe. They shook more when the doorbell rang. My date was right on time.

Standing at the door with my heart pounding, I stared at the creamy white paint and hoped my face was not that pale. After one more deep breath, I opened the door and smiled. A man with thinning gray hair made eye contact with me.

"Hi, I'm Richard." His boyish grin signaled that I was in for a fun evening. Or a silly one. As he looked me up and down, there wasn't a hint of judgment on his face.

Did he hear the drumbeat of my heart? Did he know that he looked like Johnny Cash in those black pants, black shirt, and white tie? He looked better than in his picture—more animated, warm, and inviting.

My heart fluttered as I said, "I'm Lynn. Would you like to come in?"

Running his eyes up and down me one more time, he said, "We should probably go."

The approval behind the twinkle in his eyes was exhilarating. I practically floated to his car, a Mazda convertible that made him as proud as a boy with a new toy.

CHAPTER 1

I NEVER DREAMED that I would marry for the first time at age sixty-two.

When I was eighteen and getting ready for college, I read a statement from the Vassar catalogue: *If you are one of the 93% who eventually marry . . .*

The phrase, *eventually marry,* rolled off my tongue. Maybe I wasn't the only woman who wanted a career, independence, and security before marriage. Maybe my priorities weren't as odd as they seemed.

During high school, I dated exactly twice. Boys wanted to hang out with the pretty, confident girls. At five-foot-three and 165 pounds, I needed to lose weight. Dieting drove me crazy. No matter what weight loss plan I tried, my stomach growled and I couldn't concentrate. Why didn't magazines in the mid-sixties tell girls that intelligence, creativity, and confidence were attractive qualities? Why did I listen to those magazines that told me a thin body would give me success and happiness?

On both of my high school dates, I was incredibly nervous. Irrationally nervous. My mind raced, scrambling my thoughts and potential jokes until I was ready to scream. Better to keep my mouth shut and be considered a fool than to open it and remove all doubt.

I was too embarrassed to ask anyone how to act on a date. Instead, I memorized tips from *Seventeen Magazine*:

Ask him what he's interested in.
Talk about his teams—basketball, football, debate, chess . . .
Be available, but not too available.

How could I flirt without giving a guy the wrong idea? Where were the lines drawn between a nice girl and a cheap girl?

Even though I opened up a bit in college, my personal feelings remained submerged. My peers talked freely about their dates—so, I gave mixers a try. On Friday nights, the men from Williams or West Point or Yale got on a bus and rode to Vassar. In their dorms, the girls put on mini-skirts and eye shadow and we all met in a building called Students, where a local band played and the men asked the women to dance. If things went well, you spent the evening with the man who asked for the first dance, exchanged phone numbers, and he called by Wednesday to invite you to his campus the next weekend. If things didn't go well, you stood around and tried to look available and happy, or at least perky.

One night, as the women on either side of me were selected, I noticed a female techie from the drama department. Wearing a work shirt and drinking a beer, she sat on the edge of the stage, looking as lonely as I felt. Being thin and attractive didn't help her. What chance did I have? Looking happy and available didn't work. Neither did looking like your boyfriend was in Vietnam and you were just here for the music.

One night, I danced with a drunken townie, who invited me to his car. After two beers, I thought it would be fun. We settled into the backseat of his buddy's clunker. He put his lips against mine and pressed hard enough to make my teeth hurt. His tongue reached past them and circled around my tongue. One hand held my head in place while the other stroked my breast. My polyester dress was lined, but it didn't matter. My nipples stayed flat. His kisses and hot hands were gross.

A snippet from *Seventeen Magazine* raced through my mind. "If everyone else is making out, take him out to the kitchen and make him a sandwich." There was no kitchen anywhere near the car.

"'Scuse me," he blurted out, and threw the door open. I heard him retching behind the trunk. He got back in and said, "Sorry about that," before he put his mouth back on mine again.

Pushing him away, I said, "Gotta go."

"What? Why?" He squinted.

"I have to go and . . . uh . . . water my cactus." It was a line I'd heard in the dining room—guaranteed to get rid of a guy you never wanted to see again. Walking back to my dorm, I felt buzzed and repulsed. And grateful. The author of *Seventeen* would have been proud of me.

Dating soon lost its allure, so I spent Friday and Saturday nights babysitting. This was an adventure I missed out on in high school. One night, when the little ones would not go to sleep, I separated their bedroom into Donald-land and Mikey-land, and told each boy that he had to stay in his own land until morning. They giggled, and they also stayed. Babysitting gave me power, and I graduated with money in the bank and a desire to teach. Teaching came easier than dating.

In the Seventies, I ran an award-winning high school drama program, which kept me so busy that there was no time to date. I shared car rides with a man named Eric. We both commuted across the Bay Bridge to San Francisco to perform with a group called Improvisation, Inc. Eric was three years younger than me and insisted that when he found a girlfriend, she would be younger than him. Even though I wondered what his lips would feel like on mine, I couldn't ask for a kiss. Not after that statement.

In my thirties, I dated a gray-haired businessman, who lived down the hall. He refused to tell me his exact age. A gallant, sophisticated man with an ex and two children in Australia, he was ready for heavy petting as soon as we kissed. We went to dinner and the movies, and I wished he wouldn't talk down to me. When he finally realized that I would never sleep with him, he found a more willing girlfriend. She wore makeup, had short, curly hair, and dressed to accentuate her full figure. I would watch them walking hand-in-hand towards the elevator when I was supposed to be locking my apartment door. Though I should have been sad, I breathed easier. The pressure was off. By finding a more loving and expressive woman, he let me off the hook.

In the hopes of meeting someone suitable, I joined an activities group for people over forty. Most people in the group were divorced and cautious. David had never married, though. Even after the group stopped meeting, we took trips to museums and baseball games and movies. He wanted a companion who paid her own way. Like Improvisation-Inc-Eric, he was younger than me, and he, too, was seeking a relationship with a younger woman.

When I first met Warren, I was already collecting State Teacher's Retirement. We enjoyed lunch at the local diner or his favorite dim sum restaurant. His ad on Craigslist said, "Friends First." When we finally talked about going away overnight, I hesitated. How could I tell a man my age that I didn't have any experience beyond kissing? His laughter would be humiliating. So, I kept putting him off.

After two years of phone calls, lunch dates, hospital visits, and dog walks, Warren didn't call for three days. When the phone finally rang one July evening, I was driving. I saw his name and pulled into a shady parking spot at an elementary school.

Sunlight glinted off the monkey bars as I said, "Hello?"

When his son spoke, my stomach flinched. The news didn't really surprise me. Warren passed away, in the company of his best friend, Charlie, a seventy-five pound German shepherd. He left Charlie to me. I had a new responsibility in my life.

Although I wanted to keep him, there wasn't enough room in my condominium for such a large dog. Besides, I didn't have the strength to walk him and my little shih tzu, Mikko, and Mikko resisted sharing me with anyone. Reaching out to dog lovers in the San Francisco Bay Area, I settled Charlie into a good, stable home. As for me? I holed up. A year later, my loneliness slowly nudged me back onto Craigslist.

I finally met the man who would become my husband there. His ad in Men Seeking Women read:

CLASSIC
1944 classic roadster with many miles left!
Motor humms, transmission smooth and and all the gears work!
Only two previous owners, very great women.
Two tone, white with a gray top.
Seeking a new woman owner who knows how to drive a classic!
Thanks
PS, This car is at church every Sunday so if that is a problem with you this car is not for you.

Obviously, he was shopping for his third wife. Before our first date, he asked if I would ever marry *if I fell in love.*

Of course, I said yes. I would have said yes to any expectation. His questions made me feel like I was interviewing for a job. They also made me curious. Where might this go if I didn't resist? Besides, after sixty-two years of living single, it probably wasn't possible for me to fall in love. I wasn't really tricking him. I was just agreeing. Fears lingered, though.

What if I got in too deeply?

What if I became dependent?

What if he took my life savings and left?

CHAPTER 2

HOW I ADMIRED Richard's metaphor. Did he know how much he showed me? He had a clever mind, but the grammatical errors in his ad made me wonder about his level of education. Who wrote an extended metaphor with mechanical errors? Reading his ad, I felt like a snob. As a former English teacher, I noticed both the mistakes and his inviting tone. He set up a wonderfully fun pattern, though. Following it was easy. I clicked on Reply and said:

Love your ad.
I suppose I'd be a 1949 classic roadster.
Motor hums unless it hesitates. Transmission and gears probably need a road test.
Original owner.
Two-tone, white with a reddish-brown top.
This classic roadster could be parked next to yours on Sunday.
Our roads aren't, perfectly, parallel. Might make life interesting.
=) If anything piques your interest, feel free to write back.

Just a few minutes after midnight, I clicked the send button. The next morning, an email with his photo was waiting. Though he had no smile and his arms were folded across his chest, I couldn't stop grinning. He asked for a picture of me. No man had ever wanted my photo before. Not even Warren.

Within thirty minutes of sending it, his next email arrived. "Wow. You're an author! Tell me more about yourself. Where do you live, have you been married, divorced, widowed? Kids? Where do you go to church?"

I hadn't told him that I was an author. Must have noticed my signature line. Again, his questions made it easy for me to respond.

I clicked on reply and wrote, "I live in Danville, but grew up in Los Gatos and went to college in Poughkeepsie, NY. I never married, so I have no kids unless you count my aging toddler in a fur suit, Mikko McPuppers. You told me you were married twice. Any kids? Pets? Where do you go to church?"

Looking out the window in my office, I wondered what kind of complimentary closing I should use. Hoping to meet you? Keep writing? Please don't take advantage of my vulnerability? No! I put Thanks and added Lynn. Not wanting to overthink it, I hit send.

Several emails later, I discovered that he had seven adult children, including a set of twins. He worked as an electrical contractor and pastored a church on Sundays. When he asked for my phone number and a good time to call, my adrenaline surged. Suddenly, I was filled with energy, despite my sore muscles and bad leg. I typed a quick answer, reread my words, and decided that I sounded clear, as I gave him three different choices. He took the first one and called later that evening.

"Hello?"

"Lynn? It's Richard. How are you this evening?" The words were insignificant. His warm, engaging tone made me eager to talk to him. Instead of telling me all about himself, he asked questions.

"Where do you live?"

"Danville," I said, wondering if he was too nervous to remember it from my email. "Do you know where that is?"

"I've done a couple jobs out there. Where do you go to church?" he asked.

"St. Tim's. I should say St. Timothy's."

"Catholic?"

"Nope." There was an awkward pause. "I always tell people I grew up as an absentee Episcopalian."

"Absentee?"

"We didn't go to church a lot," I explained, squirming inside. I wanted to come off as clever, not stupid. "It was five miles away and there were no sidewalks, so I needed a ride to get there."

"Got it. So, you're a writer. What do you write about?"

"Lots of different things. I run an e-zine called *Writer Advice,* and I have a book out called *You Want Me to Do WHAT?* which is journaling for caregivers. And I write short pieces. And teach for Story Circle Network."

Stop before he gets bored! In my next breath, I asked him about his two wives, who had passed away, and he told me about his forty-year marriage to his first wife and his second marriage that lasted exactly three years and one day.

Then he said, "Would you like to go out for dinner on Friday?"

Like to? My hands shook like autumn leaves as I replied, "Yes, but I'm in a movie group that meets this Friday."

"How about Thursday?"

* * *

Waiting those forty-eight hours was a nightmare and a fantasy. My imagination played havoc with my rational mind. This might be only one date with a man who asked good questions and listened to my answers. Oh, how I wanted more. It was impossible not to anticipate and obsess.

CHAPTER 3

"WON'T YOU COME in?" I said.

"We should be going."

I grabbed my handbag and followed him to his Mazda.

". . . I'll be okay in a few weeks," I said, even though I had a feeling he was barely listening.

"You're just fine," he said, opening the car door.

His seats were a little lower than the ones in my car, so I struggled to get in. Closing his door, he smiled at me. "Watch this." Revving the engine, he reached up and unlatched the top. "Press that button."

"What does it do?"

"Just press it," he answered.

As the hardtop rose and folded back, he stared at me. "Want to ride with the top down?"

"Sure." I had never ridden in a convertible before.

Glancing over at me, he added, "Not worried about your hair?"

I shook my head. "I have a brush."

He set his GPS and pulled out of the driveway. Again, he glanced over at me. Not wanting to seem too anxious, I stared up at the sky.

"Tell me about your kids," I said.

"Well, one of my twins works in the business with me and . . ."

He sure did talk a lot. That day I found out a lot about his kids. Basically, that they're individuals, each living their own life. Four boys. Three girls. *What a talker!*

"Looks like a good place to park." He pulled into a spot that faced the street. Walking around the car, he opened my door. With such a low seat, I struggled to stand up.

"This seat is lower than mine," I explained.

He took my hand as we crossed the parking lot. What if he thought the limp was permanent? "I slammed into a wall in the hallway about two weeks ago, right after tripping over Mikko McPuppers," I explained. "Don't worry. My muscles are almost healed."

"That's okay. I'm used to taking care of my wives."

Did that mean what I thought it meant? With my mind twirling, I stared straight ahead.

"Guess I shouldn't have said it that way," he added. "What I meant was that I'm already comfortable with you."

"It's okay," I replied. "You're easy to talk to."

"Have you ever been here before?" he asked.

"A few times."

"On a date?"

"With my mother, I think." I glance around at the wooden walls and hanging Western art. "It's been a long time. And once, on a Friday night, I came in and sold some raffle tickets for a moped. We were raising money because we were selected to perform at the International Thespian Society's Festival."

Once we had a chance to look at the menus he said, "I suggest the rib eye. Very juicy. Besides, I have a two-for-one coupon, and I can use it if you order the same meal as me."

"I don't usually eat red meat," I said, smiling. "But I'll try it."

He leaned across the table and added, "I'm going to have steak soup and a baked potato for my sides."

"I'll have a baked potato, too," I said, reading down the menu. "And . . . um, broccoli."

"Do you want a cocktail?" he asked.

"No thanks."

"It's okay if you want one."

"I don't drink anymore," I explained, keeping it simple.

Nodding, he grinned. "I don't drink much either. I have to be available whenever the phone rings. How about coffee or a soft drink?"

"Water, I suppose."

"Then I'll have coffee."

After the server brought our drinks and took our orders, he leaned across the table again. "I'm going to play a trick on the waitress." Resting his spoon against the inside edge of his cup so that it stood straight up inside the coffee, he laughed. "Silly, I know. It's a trick a long-time friend taught me."

The server walked back over and asked if everything was okay.

Richard winked at me, and replied, "Got any coffee that isn't so strong?"

Standing prim and proper in her scoop-neck top, the waitress looked puzzled.

"He's kidding," I said, laughing.

"How did you do that?" the prim woman asked.

He showed her, and she left shaking her head. Richard might be fun, once I get used to his sense of humor.

"This is going pretty well so far, don't you think?" he asked.

Smiling, I nodded.

"You reckon you'd like to drive up the coast together on Saturday?" he asked.

Like to? Try love. My heart soared. We weren't even done with the first date and he was asking for a second. Thirty years earlier, I had the same thrilling burst of energy when I went onstage at Improvisation, Inc. Anything could happen in unscripted theatre, and real life was even better.

When the bill came, he paid with the coupon he clipped and a gift card he received on Father's Day. Frugal and sensible. I liked that. We had something in common.

"I only received two Father's Day gifts," he said, as he set the coupon inside the bill holder.

"Did that bother you?"

Smiling, he shook his head. "My kids are adults. They have their own lives."

Driving back to Danville, we kept the top down. The stars sparkled above my head, and I would never forget that dome of a sky, even if nothing came of this night.

"Would you like to come in for coffee?" I asked as I unlocked my door.

"What kind do you have?"

"Folgers Instant. I'll put the water on."

"Instant coffee?" He was incredulous. With a shake of his head he added, "I don't drink instant. Let me see what I can figure out." Walking straight into my kitchen, he opened one cabinet after another, while I worried. How long had it been since I cleaned or even straightened them?

"Let me find something," I offered, though I still wondered what was wrong with instant coffee.

"That's all right. I'll take care of it." For all I knew, he did this with all of his dates. How could he be so confident in my kitchen? I hated searching for the right pot or food container in someone else's kitchen. To me, it felt like invading someone's space. So why was Richard right at home?

Against my better judgment, I left him alone, though I could still see most of what he was doing from my couch. The teakettle pinged as it hit the stove. A few minutes later, Richard walked into the living room holding two mugs of Lipton tea. I grabbed coasters.

"I drink coffee all day and night," he said. "It calms me down."

Calming down with caffeine was a common symptom of ADHD.

I wasn't ready to tell him that. If he had that condition, I would recognize it soon enough. I'd been trained to look for it in an adult literacy program where I worked ten years earlier. Instead of talking about how caffeine affected people, I asked, "Do you still want to drive up the coast on Saturday, like we talked about at dinner?"

"I think so." My heart dropped. "I have to call to another woman I've been talking to, but we went out first, so it shouldn't be a problem."

My heart soared again. Riding this emotional roller coaster took me back to my adolescence, when hope and angst fought inside of me. I wasn't a teenager seeking praise anymore. I had become stable. At least that's what I told myself.

When he said, I should be going, and set his cup on the coaster, I was startled. I wanted to know more about him and his family and his business and his church. The night had flown past, and our cups were empty.

He stared straight ahead as we walked to the door. My looking at him made no difference. Running my tongue slowly across the soft, wet inside of my upper lip did not give him the hint I intended. I wanted a kiss. He remained oblivious. *Men!*

Walking out my front door he said, "Good night," without even looking at me.

Didn't dates normally end in a kiss if all went well?

"Do you really think he'll call?" I asked Mikko as I closed the door.

Mikko gnawed on an old bone. He hadn't even barked when Richard first arrived, or when we returned. That was a sign of his trust, and he did not trust easily. Glancing in the mirror over my fireplace, I sighed. What did I do wrong? As soon as I asked myself that question, a quick fix came into my mind.

My steak sat in a Styrofoam box in his trunk. Even if I never saw him again, I wanted that steak. He had pursued me most of the evening. Why not pursue my steak?

The warm night air felt good on my skin as I went down the steps and across the path, hoping he'd still be there. Richard sat in his car with the top down. Holding an unlit cigarette in one hand and his lighter in the other, he stared into the darkness. Warren had been a smoker. So had my father. Personally, I didn't like the habit, but my sense of smell had never worked. This was not a deal-breaker for me.

Was he waiting until the top was down to smoke? That would mean he didn't want the odor stinking up his car.

"Good," I said. "You're still here. I forgot my steak."

He popped the trunk, and I removed the Styrofoam box with my name on it.

"Glad you came back," he said, still holding the unlit cigarette.

"Me too." Another big grin spread across my face and up into my cheeks.

"You look very kissable standing there."

"Maybe I am." His smiling eyes encouraged me to keep going. "Maybe you'll find out one of these days."

My toes tingled as he replied, "I'd like that."

Standing next to the passenger door, his eyes twinkled again. Flirting with Richard was going to be fun. Could he tell that I wanted a man in my life? That I wanted to know what every other woman and half the teenagers in the world already knew? Did he have any idea how badly I wanted to feel normal instead of unlovable?

If I never saw him again, at least the memory of this moment would be mine.

It should have been enough, but was it?

CHAPTER 4

BEFORE OPENING MY eyes the next morning, my mind drifted through all the different possibilities. Why didn't Richard kiss me? He made it clear that he wanted more than a platonic relationship. So did I, though I was afraid to say so out loud. Maybe losing Warren to cancer prepared me for a relationship with Richard.

Talking with Warren was easy as long as the subject was his German shepherd, Charlie, or the passengers on the AC Transit bus he drove, or even Linda, his second wife. After all, his ad had said, *Friends first. If more materializes, I'm open. If not, you can never have too many friends.*

Warren mostly emailed or called me. Once he made me feel safe, I agreed to meet in a hole-in-the-wall café—his description, not mine. As soon as I entered and looked around, he spotted me. Although we never exchanged photos, he waved at me. His sincere smile sent ripples of gratification all through me. He looked a little like a pale version of the actor Sam Elliott.

Spending time with Warren was good. For me, it was more fun than being with David. We laughed as we compared our dogs, our activities, and our lives. I never laughed as much with David. After lunch in that small café, I offered to pay my half. Cocking his head to one side, Warren said, "I always treat my dates."

Was he acting old fashioned? Yes.

Did it bother me? Not really. As long as he wasn't buying more than lunch. When did I become so distrustful? More importantly, would it stop?

After lunch, Warren walked me to my car.

"You have a limp," I said as he pulled open the door.

"Neuropathy," he replied, "both feet."

"Oh?" Was I being rude? Should I apologize?

"Probably from the chemo," he added.

"Cancer?" I asked, then wished that I hadn't.

"Pancreatic."

A blue *Disabled* placard hung on his rearview mirror. I should have known. Made me appreciate my legs and feet, even though I already wobbled and lurched when I lost my balance. At fifty-nine, I had fibromyalgia, but the symptoms were mostly under control.

Once home, I googled neuropathy: A condition that caused tingling, numbness, and weakness in the arms and legs. Warren walked slowly, as if his body were made of dry twigs. Made me fear that a stiff breeze would knock him over before he got into his Volvo.

The following week, we met for lunch again. And the one after that. Usually, we visited his favorite dim sum restaurant, though we tried a number of hole-in-the-wall cafés scattered throughout the county. Afterwards, I often follow him back to his home in Martinez. Sitting on his patio, I talked while he threw a grungy tennis ball across the grass. Charlie always brought it back.

Not like Mikko. With Mikko, if you threw it, you fetched it. When he came with me, Mikko enjoyed licking the food off the wall above Charlie's food bowl. No chasing a stupid tennis ball around a yard for him. Such different dogs—just like their owners.

September 11 was a special day, Warren's birthday. By then he was willing to let me treat him to lunch. As I paid, though, Warren kept glancing at the bill. He wasn't comfortable with my paying for him.

"Want to walk the dogs?" I asked as we walked out of the restaurant.

"Sure." He opened the door for me, and said, "Let's go."

After sitting in the car for an hour, our dogs were ready to walk. Mikko was on a leash. Charlie stuck close to Warren, who kept him under complete control through his voice. We circled a couple of times while the dogs sniffed and did their business. Neither of us could walk very far, so after a couple of trips around the parking lot, we put our dogs back inside the vehicles. While we stood between our cars, I looked up at Warren and said, "Can I give you a birthday kiss?"

Warren's eyes widened like a deer caught in the headlights. Classic. I didn't mean to embarrass him. How I wished a hole would open up and swallow me. Just then he smiled and said, "Okay." His fear was gone.

Placing his hands on my shoulders, he drew me towards him. Our lips met. There was as much hunger in his kiss as in mine. When it was over, I looked into his eyes—or tried. He stared at his shoes.

How could I make it right?

Without speaking, Warren got into his car, with Charlie in the passenger seat, and drove away. Sliding into the driver's seat of my Camry, I glanced over at Mikko.

"Well, I guess it's just you and me. You good?"

Mikko woofed.

Driving home, I concentrated on my to-do list but my thoughts kept falling back to Warren's reaction and his silence. Hopefully, I hadn't scared him off, and he would call in a few days.

* * *

We continued to meet for lunch as fall turned to winter. The winds increased, pulling red, yellow, and orange leaves off the sycamores that lined the back roads.

Just before Christmas, we met for lunch. He surprised me with a gift-wrapped box. I slid the ribbon off with shaky hands and saw a long gold chain. "That's fourteen-carat gold," he said as I put it over my head, allowing it to drop down.

"It's beautiful." I said running my fingers over the gold links. *Jewelry?* After our kiss on his birthday, I didn't see that coming.

"Sorry this isn't more," I said as I handed him a box of See's candy. His face dropped. When I bought it, a box of candy made sense. He was so thin and it was an appropriate gift for a friend. Of course, no one replaced the love of his life, Linda. Clearly, though, he hoped for a more romantic present—something that would confirm that we felt the same way about each other. How did I miss another signal? Why was it so hard to get this right?

* * *

Because he took morphine to control his pain, Warren's medical plan required him to see a therapist once a month. He joked about it, and one day put his arm around my shoulder as we walked from the parking lot and into my favorite restaurant. Did his therapist suggest it after he told her about the disparity in our Christmas presents and show me how he felt to build up my trust? Apparently, no one involved had thought about our unsteady gaits; we hip-bumped each other with every step. And wavered. And giggled. Bonded by shared challenges

A week later, he asked if I ever heard of Shadowbrook, a place near Santa Cruz with a brook running through the restaurant. "We could have dinner and spend the night," he suggested.

I got way too quiet for a phone call.

"We could have one room with two beds," he offered.

"Um . . ." The words wouldn't come out. Though it sounded like a reasonable compromise, I didn't know what was implied.

Or I knew exactly what was implied and was afraid.

Until he was told the truth, going away with him implied a promise that I could not fulfill. Virginity hung over me like an unwanted fog bank. I couldn't see through it. I never even thought about what my silence suggested to Warren.

* * *

A couple weeks later, the fire chief in Brooktrails passed away. Brooktrails was where Warren lived with Linda, adopted Charlie, and became a volunteer firefighter. Because he was a good friend of the chief, he was going to the funeral and invited me to go along. Again, he said we could have one room with two beds. He wanted company. How could I tell him what kept racing through my mind? I had no sexual experience. And there was the Linda factor. Would being with me make him feel disloyal to her—especially if we were in Brooktrails?

"I don't think I can go. I can take care of Charlie," I offered as a compromise.

"Charlie is coming with me." His voice was cold and sharp.

As soon as we hung up, I called my wise friend, Stacy.

"Lynn, he's asking for your support," she explained.

"True."

"This is about him—not you. He doesn't want to go through this alone."

"You're right. It's not about me. Thanks."

I took a deep breath and called to tell him that I had changed my mind.

Although I had ridden in his Volvo many times, I was nervous as we headed north on the day before the funeral. No way could I change my mind and come back that night. We drove under the green Willits sign arching across the main street and pulled into a little motel with a Western theme. After he registered us for one room with two beds, we picked up a service-dog vest for Charlie at the fire station. The next step? Visiting the huge warehouse where the service and reception would be held.

When we walked in, we saw people setting up tables for the buffet that would follow the memorial service the next day. One woman glowed when she saw Warren with Charlie and his new friend, me. An older man said, "I hoped you'd come back for this. And who's the little lady?" Whenever he introduced me, I glowed with pride.

Later we drove to the Brooktrails Resort just outside of Willits. My family stayed there once when I was twelve. As we drove up the steep hill, the pine needles and the curves in the road were unchanged. I was twelve again. Also sixty-two.

We crossed the wooden porch of the lodge and peered through a dusty window into the bar. Warren's wife had waitressed there, and for a moment, we were lost in our separate pasts.

Next, we drove down the dirt road to the cabins. So much had changed that I couldn't tell where my family had once stayed. Warren swung the Volvo onto an unfamiliar road. We drove past his old house. He explained that Charlie had been free to roam the hills leash-free and always came home for supper.

After our own supper, we settled into our room for the night. Warren took the bed by the door and Charlie hopped up on it. Next, he lifted my suitcase onto the luggage rack, turned on the TV, and disappeared into the bathroom to change into hospital scrubs, which were his pajamas. When he emerged, I noticed his ghostly-pale feet. There was space between his toes and I could almost see the bones in them.

He turned down the TV and we chitchatted about his life in Brooktrails, and my memories of a tiny creamery where my family went for sodas when we vacationed there. Then he said, "Did you bring something to sleep in?"

Feeling my cheeks flush, I replied, "Yes." I stood up and pulled out a purple top with a lacy v-neck, and some black pajama bottoms.

I had purchased them the day before. Adrenaline pounding, I went into the bathroom and changed. My drooping nipples pressed against the soft shirt. I sucked in the flab hanging above my waist, ran a comb through my hair, and returned, carrying my clothes in front of me.

Warren took one look and said, "It looks like you're wearing sweats."

"Sweats? The bottoms are silk," I said. And what about your scrubs, I could have added, but I didn't. Instead, I stashed my clothes in my suitcase, pulled back the covers, and sat with my legs pulled up and my arms crossed in an attempt to hide my nipples.

"You can come and sit by me, if you want to." Charlie, who was lying next to Warren, looked up.

"Your bed is kind of full." I silently thanked Charlie.

He looked at my crossed arms and said, "Or you can stay there. We can just talk." And that is exactly what we did until it was time to turn out the lights and get some sleep.

When we awoke, Charlie was curled around my feet. "That's never happened before," Warren said.

He never asked why I wouldn't come over, and I didn't know how to tell him.

After the memorial service in a warehouse where the sound system echoed off the high ceiling, we ate from the enormous buffet and got back in his car for the return trip. We were still friends, but not friends with benefits. Neither of us talked about that night again.

We continued to go out to lunch, and on Valentine's Day he treated me to dinner at a Chinese restaurant where I often picked up take-out for him. When we left the restaurant, a half moon was shining down. As we turned onto his street a few blocks later, Andy Williams crooned "Moon River" on the oldies station. The surging melody took me back to the summer when I was thirteen. I wanted a boyfriend so badly. Listening to the familiar strains, I thought, this isn't what I had imagined, but it's not bad.

I was with a man who respected me. Though the ins and outs of love remained a mystery, I cared about Warren. Going out to dinner on Valentine's Day with him would always be a cherished memory.

Four months later, he succumbed to cancer. Or maybe he was worn out from fighting it. Did the distinction matter? I was alone again.

CHAPTER 5

AS A HIGH school teacher, I taught Langston Hughes' poem, "A Dream Deferred." My dream of getting married and raising a family was definitely deferred. Then it died. According to Hughes, a new dream can rise out of the ashes. Would Richard be my Phoenix? When my cell rang the Saturday morning after our first date, I was checking emails.

Richard asked, "Are you up?" in a chipper voice.

I looked down at my nightshirt. "Kind of."

"You remember the other woman we talked about? Well, I told her we had dinner and I wanted to see how things worked out." I loved that he was a man of his word. Unfortunately, his control issues, from the rib eye to the coffee, bothered my feminist streak. It was too early to tell whether this was friendship, infatuation, or something deeper. I had never spent time with a man who was so clear about what he wanted and how he would get it. "I thought we could start the day early," Richard continued.

"Okay. Where are you?" How quickly could I shower and throw on clothes and makeup?

"In Danville. I just got off on Diablo Road."

My heart sank. He was only five minutes away. So, I told him the truth: "I have to shower and dress."

"I don't mind waiting. I'll bring coffee."

After the fastest shower in history, I threw on jeans, a summer t-shirt, and my Nikes. I was rubbing my hair with a towel when the doorbell rang. He was bright-eyed and eager, standing there with a Starbucks cup in each hand and a goofy grin on his face.

When we turned east onto Ygnacio Valley Road a few minutes later I asked, "Weren't we were heading for the coast?"

"I'm taking you to Black Bear for breakfast."

"In Walnut Creek?"

"It's on Bancroft." I thought the nearest Black Bear was in Gilroy. "So, you went to the University of Pennsylvania, right?" he asked, making conversation.

"No." He must have been confusing me with another woman. How many had he talked to in his quest to find his new wife?

"I thought you said . . ."

"No." Pause. Silence. "I didn't say." How would he feel about dating a Vassar graduate? The silence was unbearable. He could be imagining anything. "Since you asked, I got my BA from Vassar."

"Isn't that somewhere around Pennsylvania?"

"New York. It's a good school. College was a long time ago." Before he could ask about graduate school or occupations, I said, "What about you?"

"I have an associate of applied science in electronics technology from Del Mar College in Corpus Christi, and attended California Christian College in Fresno with my first wife, Jean." The answer sounded practiced. As time went on I would find out that he was married before he went to the Christian college, and Jean took notes while he slept with his eyes open. At least, that's how he described it.

She was raising kids. He was working full time and going to school. No wonder he fell asleep on the road one night. Though no one was hurt, he took the warning to heart and dropped out of school. Clearly, he made the right choice. But how does a pastor run a church without a degree? I didn't want to sound pushy or touch on a sensitive area, so I put that on my mental list of questions to ask later.

* * *

As always, the meals at Black Bear were humongous, and we both left food on our plates. Normally, I would have wrapped my leftover biscuit in a couple of napkins and taken it home. Today, I hesitated. I didn't want Richard to think I was cheap or stingy.

When the bill came I reached for it. "You treated last night."

A warm smile lit his face. "You just met one of my requirements. You're willing to pay."

Since I always took care of myself and was good at it, I was delighted to find a man who appreciated that. I pulled two twenties from my wallet.

"Want me to take that up to the cashier?" he asked as I sipped my coffee. When he came back, he took a generous tip out of my change and handed me what was left. What a weird combination of kindness and control.

Back in his Mazda he lowered the roof, then looked into my eyes and said, "So you've never been married, right?"

"Right."

"Have you had boyfriends?"

"I've had friends that were men."

"Exactly how close have you gotten to a man?" he asked.

"A long time ago there was an older man. We . . . uh . . . kissed a lot."

"You've never been intimate?" He said it without the slightest hint of judgment.

Shaking my head, I stared straight ahead. No way could I look at him. When he didn't respond, I had no choice but to say something.

"No."

And just like that, the dreaded truth was out. I was sixty-two and had never been intimate. The shame was overwhelming.

Richard asked the right question, and I was totally comfortable answering honestly. Not only that, he didn't ask why, or what was wrong with me.

I was curious about sex—also terrified. What would he think when he saw me naked and touched places that have always been private? Why was I afraid of something that came naturally to others? Richard had saved me from the silence that Warren and I imposed on each other. I wasn't ready to jump in bed with anyone—not even the most non-judgmental man I had ever met.

Growing up in the late Fifties, I was taught rules. Sex had consequences. Sex before marriage could ruin the woman's life forever. Even though Richard had told me that he was looking for a woman who'd been married before, he was not repulsed by my answer. I didn't realize I'd been holding my breath until I exhaled in a slow, quiet whoosh.

"I know it's unusual. I've just never let anybody get that close." I couldn't leave his unspoken question hanging between us.

He reached across the stick shift, put his hand on my arm and said, "Maybe you were saving yourself all these years for me."

My feminist-self rose to the surface. How I wanted to roll my eyes. But for all I knew, he could be right. He showed me a unique mixture of confidence, genuine warmth, and chauvinism, and he didn't see any clash there.

* * *

We drove north on Interstate 680, turned west on Highway 37, which took us above grassy waterways, and continued until we came to Route 101. By the time we were driving up the coast, the Mazda's swaying had made me lightheaded. Breathing in the salt air as the waves crashed against the shore below didn't fix the problem. Even though I wanted to be the perfect date, my queasy stomach kept messing with my goals.

"Can you pull over when it's easy?" I asked.

He wasn't upset at all, and I loved that. Swinging abruptly into the first driveway about a hundred yards up the road, he pulled to a stop. I opened my door and headed up the dirt road, away from the ocean. Halfway up the path, Richard put his arm around me. We stopped walking at a green metal fence with California's golden summer grass on the other side. There, in the coastal breeze, he turned me towards him and put both arms around me. Their weight felt good. Stabilizing. His eyes twinkled as he looked into mine and his lips formed the most enchanting smile. Then he cocked his head and I closed my eyes. And . . . he kissed me.

Hoping he wanted a deep kiss, I opened my mouth slightly. When he didn't take the initiative, I allowed my tongue to slide into his mouth. An older man taught me how to do this as I was leaving a cast party after one of our college shows closed.

"That was nice," Richard said after the kiss ended.

What a relief after Warren's birthday kiss.

"You don't have to use your tongue so much," Richard continued.

Ouch! From the glow on his face, I could tell that he liked it. So why was he correcting me? How was I supposed to please him?

And why was I thinking this way? Since when did I try to reshape myself to meet a man's expectations? If I cared what he thought, was I falling in love? Could it happen that quickly?

The tingling on my lips and in my mouth kept me from taking his criticism seriously. Maybe he was giving me options or trying to decrease the pressure I felt. Giving me suggestions for improvement was certainly better than saying nothing.

* * *

Later that day, we made our way inland across River Road, which runs through the Russian River resort country. Sitting in the passenger seat, I tilted my head back and stared up at the leafy tree branches arching across the road. Richard glanced over and asked, "So, you're a Christian?"

His question somewhat surprised me because we were just in the middle of our second date. Growing up, my parents said that we were charter members of Saint Andrew's Church. However, we rarely attended services. I was baptized when I was a baby and confirmed when I was a sixth grader. For three years before I met Richard, I attended the local Episcopal Church. Sitting in the back, I was comfortably anonymous. Perhaps I came for the rituals, the music, or some deep need I could not label.

"Yes," I said.

"Have you been saved?" he asked.

Although Episcopalians do not expect members of the congregation to be born again, I had accepted Christ twice. Once in the privacy of my living room during the last week of a difficult school year, and again in the office of a massage therapist who was an assertive Christian. No one knew about either time. I replied with, "Yes."

"Do you remember when and where?"

"Lying on the table in my cranial sacral therapist's office."

"That's good," he replied. "What were the words you said?"

I didn't memorize them. His inquisition made me very uncomfortable.

"Dunno," I said with a casual shrug. "I only heard them once. Maybe if you say them, they'll ring a bell." The cynical part of me considered this a trick. He got about five or six words out before I said, "That's it!" Hearing the sinner's prayer from the man I kissed an hour earlier made me squirm. Even though I was embarrassed, his straightforward manner still appealed to me. If he had a question, he asked it. So far, he hadn't said or asked anything that was a real deal-breaker.

Apparently, being saved was a prerequisite for marriage. His second wife, Joan, had been saved shortly before the wedding. I always thought that you were saved because you wanted Jesus in your life. If there was any discrepancy in Joan's motivation, Richard never saw it. Instead, he asked, "Have you been baptized?"

"When I was a baby."

"Sprinkled or dunked?"

"Sprinkled."

"That doesn't count." He watched the road as he said it. If he had looked over, he would have seen so much disbelief on my face that he might have run into a redwood tree and crumpled his car.

"It counts in the Episcopal Church, especially once you're confirmed."

"I can't marry a woman who isn't a Christian," he said as if he hadn't heard me. "The Bible says, 'Do not be unequally yoked in the world.'" He was giving me the facts in his down-to-earth way. I couldn't fight the beliefs of a pastor, especially on our second date.

We each had a higher power called God, even if our religious rituals and histories were different. I couldn't help asking, "Aren't we talking about rituals rather than spiritual principles?"

"I couldn't say." Was that compromise I heard in his voice? "But I accept you as a Christian," he added after a moment. Another hurdle crossed.

His interrogation almost felt like an interview for the job of a pastor's wife. What would the job entail? He had an agenda, while I only had a desire for a long-term relationship. Maybe that would have bothered a more experienced woman. However, his attention was winning me over.

We rode on, each lost in our own thoughts. Half an hour later we crossed the Carquinez Bridge. I looked at the cloudless blue sky and the boats that dotted the strait below. With the wind blowing my hair back, I enjoyed feeling desirable. Maybe we could travel the strait in a boat of our own someday, and I could see the river, with its wooden piers and grassy banks, from a new perspective.

Richard got off on Willow Road. Though I thought he might be taking me to his house, he wanted to show me his church first.

CHAPTER 6

RICHARD AND I passed empty storefronts as we drove down Willow Avenue.

"Cleo has an attitude," he said as he passed Seventh Street. Earlier he told me that he named his GPS Cleo, after a woman he dated briefly. "When I was living over on Second, she didn't like my route. She'd say, 'Turn on Second, Turn on Second! *Turn* on *Second*!' Turning on First and looping around was more than she could handle."

What do you say when someone complains about a GPS?

Glad you stayed strong?

Sorry she was so bossy?

"She's very determined, isn't she?" came out of me as we turned.

Cleo barked out, "Turn on Second!" Such a biting voice.

Richard parked facing a tan, brick building. The glass on the arched front windows was painted white, and the sashes were brown. From a distance, they looked like narrow crosses.

As I stepped out of his car, Richard said, "Take your hat off."

For a minute, I thought he was talking to himself. Some women still covered their heads in the Episcopal Church.

When I didn't respond he repeated, "Take it off," with more insistence.

He sounded like his GPS. I left the hat on the front seat, he unlocked the door, and I followed him in, aware that the issue of the hat was a difference in customs and nothing more. I picked my battles, and this wasn't one of them, despite his sharp voice.

The sanctuary walls were pale plum, and there was water damage in the right-hand corner and bits of peeling paint curling along the sidewalls. A large wooden cross hung behind the pulpit.

About ten rows of wooden pews with red cushions, separated by a center aisle, faced the front. Sunlight streamed across the ones towards the back, fading the red fabric. No altar. No candles. I could see how much Richard loved being in charge of this domain. To him, it was homey. He was a father, a leader, a pastor, and the CEO of his company. No matter where he was, he was the man in charge.

"Would you like to come to services tomorrow?" he asked, breaking into my thoughts about his leadership role. "We have Bible study at ten and preaching at eleven."

"I'll try to come for preaching."

Bible study was a label that conjured images of righteous Christians debating. It intimidated me. Or repulsed me. I wasn't sure which. When I visited churches, I liked sneaking in unobtrusively and being a fly on the wall.

The next morning, following Richard's instructions, I took I-680 to Highway 4, got off on Willow, drove past Starbucks, Burger King, and the ramp for I-80 North. At the next street sign, I wasn't on Willow anymore. I was on Parker. So I made a U-turn and drove up and down the same portion of the street three times. Just as I was about to give up and go home, my cell rang.

"Hello?" My voice was rushed and breathy.

"It's Richard. Are you coming?"

"I'm trying, but Willow keeps turning into Parker." According to my dashboard clock, I was already seven minutes late.

"That's okay," he said, chuckling. "Keep coming. Turn left on First Street and go down one block. I'll wait out front for you."

Three minutes later, I slid my Camry into a parking spot in front of the church. Richard was standing next to a young woman with a post-partum belly holding a baby carrier.

"This is Christine," he said.

"It's great to have you here." She shook my hand with her free one.

I peeked in at her tiny, sleeping baby. "Who's the little one?"

"This is Kimberley. She's eleven weeks old." Such love flowed through her voice. She beamed with pride.

Inside, the congregation—all fifteen of them—chatted across the aisles. Were we in a mall, or a park, or one of my sophomore English classes? The noise sounded like a family reunion or a picnic in a park. Church for ADHD people? I wasn't being condescending, and I didn't say it aloud. All this chatting in church was new to me. They acted as close as any family.

Would I fit in?

Did I want to?

Richard walked down the center aisle without a processional hymn or clerical robes and stood behind his pulpit. He asked the congregation to pick a hymn and we sang without a piano, a guitar, or even a pitch pipe. A new meaning for making a joyful noise popped into my head long before the song ended.

"Please stand for opening prayer. Dave, will you lead us?"

When we were seated again, he looked straight at me and asked, "Do we have anyone who is new today?"

"That would be me. I'm a friend of Richard's." Everybody turned. Most smiled.

"Make sure you introduce yourself to her and show her how friendly we are. Do we have another song?"

The hymns were straight out of movie scenes set in an old country church. I wanted to sing out, like I had in my high school choir. The best I could do was to blend my voice with the others.

After the singing, Richard asked, "Does anyone have a testimony?"

A full-figured woman asked for prayers for a daughter who was living on the street. Another woman whose voice was laced with stress asked us to pray for her migraines to stop. A man announced that he'd been clean and sober for ninety days and everyone applauded. In my church, we prayed for our government's leaders and peace. This was much more specific.

When the testimonies were over, Richard reached inside the pulpit for the collection plate. "Are there any birthdays this week?"

Someone called out, "It's not September yet."

Everybody laughed as he walked down the aisle. I tried to put my offering in the plate, but he whispered, "You do it when I come back up." So many differences in procedures.

During his message, I remembered listening to student speakers and imagined a checklist.

Eye contact? Good.

Relaxed? Yes.

Too relaxed? No. No slouching.

Diction? Pretty good. No slurring. Occasional Texas accent. His tone was more sincere than commanding.

Sincerity. Excellent! Ten out of ten.

Organization? I didn't know. I was unconsciously judging his delivery and ignoring his content. Only his sincerity stood out. I had to listen better next time.

At the end of the message, he invited people to come to the altar to pray. I was not familiar with that custom either, and stayed in my seat near the back of the church. Once we were dismissed, people stopped at my pew to talk. Three members mentioned that the church had been without a pastor's wife for nearly two years, and two others said that they hoped I'd be back. How could I resist all this acceptance?

After the service, Richard invited me to have lunch at his home. He put the top down on his Mazda, and I followed him for three blocks. He turned into a trailer park and shut off the engine. I pulled in beside him, breathing deeply. *Stay open,* I whispered as I got out of the car. He lived in a nineteen-foot fifth wheel trailer with dusty steps.

Once I followed him in, I stood in the doorway while he cleared a space for me on the couch. There were dishes in the sink and dirt on the floor. Okay, he needed a wife. However, I wasn't about to scrub those unsoaked dishes. No way.

He saw me looking around and said, "After my second wife died, one of my sons suggested I move in here to save money."

"Sounds like a plan."

A talented high school actor I once worked with spent a good part of her junior year with her new boyfriend, a twenty-year-old mechanic, living in a tiny apartment in Concord. She was on an adventure that took her out of upscale Danville. Now, so was I. But I was not sixteen anymore. Why is this man holding my interest when his trailer should be broadcasting big warning signals?

Part of me realized that we had nothing in common. A larger part of me was falling for his interest and attention. I didn't want to be dependent on anyone, and his flattery seemed like a throwback to an earlier era. On the other hand, I didn't judge people by their dirty dishes and wasn't about to start now.

Richard nuked a frozen potpie, cleared the tiny Formica table, and split the food on two Corning Ware plates. While he blessed it, I imagined myself by the green fence with the waves crashing below. Will he kiss me again?

"Why don't you sit on the sofa while I clear this away?" Richard suggested, once we finished the potpie that he called a TV dinner.

"Would you like some help?" I wasn't offering to do all the dishes stacked in his sink and on his stove. If he asked me to, I would know what he expected of his women. I wanted a partnership—not housekeeper status.

"I'll take care of it. You sit on the sofa," he said again.

Clear. Simple. Easy. He found space for the two plates and forks in the sink already crowded with other dirty dishes. He didn't rinse them, much less wash them.

When we drove up the coast the day before, he told me all about the Russian lady he dated right before me. She brought her sister on the church campout as a chaperone, and they rode up in his work truck, which he also used to haul his fifth wheel. She had told him you can't expect a lady to ride in a mess like this. You need to find a car wash with a vacuum cleaner.

"So, I stopped at a self-serve car wash outside of Guerneville," he said. "And that woman took handfuls of my papers and spread them out on the ground. I was so embarrassed."

Make that mortified, I thought, when I heard his tone.

"Everything spread on the ground and all mixed together. No one had ever done anything like that before."

Since his truck doubled as a branch office, the receipts, bills, and licenses he carried weren't trash. He had more of them Scotch-taped to the walls of his trailer. I sat on the narrow sofa and looked at post-its, state and county licenses, and a few *thank-you* cards taped to the walls and cabinet doors around me. He'd been in business thirty-one years, so whatever he was doing worked for him.

"She shouldn't have done that," I said, making a mental note not to straighten anything without being asked.

"You reckon'?" Loved the grin that came with his question. He handed me a cup of coffee as he sipped his own. Remembering his constant need for caffeine, I now believed that his brain was wired the same way as those who have ADHD. Maybe that explained the chaos in his truck.

Because he was unique in so many other ways, I decided he had a filing system that only he understood. It didn't matter if I never figured it out. I wasn't seeking a job in his company. My own work was more than enough to keep me busy.

"May I sit next to you?" he asked.

"Sure." I didn't want him to have to sit alone at the table. Besides, I was hoping for another kiss.

CHAPTER 7

RICHARD KISSED ME. It was as luscious as a summer fruit. It was the kiss that I dreamed of. His hand moved down, stroking my arm, gently. Men had done this before. Though it was supposed to feel good, it was a complete turn off. My nerve endings scraped against the inside of my skin and screamed. A side effect of fibromyalgia? Unable to tolerate the grating, I pulled away.

He slid forward on the sofa and, sitting on the edge of the cushion, he turned to see my face. "What's the matter?"

"Nothing. It just feels funny."

"It's supposed to feel good."

Duh. How can I explain that my nerve endings hate being touched? Besides, he's sitting with one cheek perched on the couch and the other hanging in the air. There has to be a better way.

Hoping to change the subject, I said, "You look awfully uncomfortable. Do you need more room?" We both looked around the crammed combination living room and kitchen. The trailer was nineteen feet end-to-end.

He pointed towards the loft. "Upstairs?" We both heard the mixture of hesitation and desire as he said it. Upstairs was a loft big enough for a full mattress. Nothing more. He knew what was implied in his words and so did I. He was a pastor. Then again, he was also a man.

Do you mean . . . ? *No.*

Are you asking me to . . . ? *No.*

Isn't a little soon for . . . ?

Nothing was right.

Although I could have said *you misunderstood,* it didn't occur to me. Did he hear a craving for attention and affection in my voice? I meant to stifle it.

I said nothing.

Neither did he. Instead he removed his shoes and socks. He looked over and grinned as he pulled the second sock off. How could I stop this? On the other hand, if not now, when? Fear and anticipation both fought to control me.

He climbed up. He rustled around for a few seconds before asking, "You coming?"

"Sure." Didn't sound sure. On the other side of the wall, he waited.

I removed one shoe. Then the other. No socks. No more stalling. A woman can say no at any time, I read once.

Pushing myself off the top step, I turned and sat on the edge of the loft. Behind Richard, who was lying on the side closest to the opening, was a yellow curtain, torn at the hem and burned by the sun. It covered the window behind his head. I was more afraid of touching that ripped and dust-laden curtain than of touching him. Outside, a July breeze stirred his wind chimes.

I sat with my back against the far wall while he explained that there were many ways to show affection with a touch or a caress. My breathing deepened and slowed. This wasn't going to be a jumping-into-bed horror story after all. This would be a lesson in the early stages of expressing love. I would let him be the instructor, knowing that I could ask him to stop whenever it seemed necessary.

He wasn't laughing or judging me as he showed me how to give and receive tenderness. "Each woman is different," he told me.

"But I'm—"

"And I'm not comparing you to anyone," he insisted.

Had he read my mind? How could I measure up to the wife who gave him seven children, or the one who rescued him from loneliness?

"You're fine," he assured me.

After a mini-course in Touching 101, I told him that I had to get home. Mikko was waiting for his food and walk. Weak excuse. However, I wasn't ready to go further. Rather than push me, he accepted my decision like a gentleman.

* * *

The next morning when I woke up, Richard, his mattress, and the torn, yellow curtain were on my mind. We had moved past his stroking my arm and found ways to touch each other that felt good. We explored. How can I be drawn to a man who lives in a trailer and never does his dishes? Does his gentle caring make up for the negatives?

I poured a cup of coffee, noticed that my pot had brown coffee residue clinging to its sides, and carried my cup across the stained living room carpet. I sat at my computer and noticed how much dust had accumulated in my office. Why was I judging his housekeeping?

Opening my email, I found a note from Richard with the subject "Good Morning!"

> *I hope you slept well and woke up with a smile on your face. I DID!*
>
> *Something has happened to me that I have been*

praying for and never could have dreamed could happen. I hope you feel the same way!

If you don't feel this way, let me down easy and fast, don't let me suffer.

Love
Richard

He signed it love. If love was a mixture of an unrelenting smile and a churning stomach, then I loved him, too. Tell me more, I wanted to say without sounding like a tease or a flirt.

Men usually ignored me, so the last part of his request surprised me. Letting him down, easily or hard, had not occurred to me. Why break up when we're just getting started?

Wait a minute. That's not what he said. He wasn't asking for that at all. He was protecting himself from hurt. Just like me. Maybe we had more in common than I realized.

Driving down tree-lined streets on my way to the grocery store, thoughts of Richard spun through my head. He'd been very forthright as he shared his family history. Did he skip a few things? There must have been all kinds of details and facts he hadn't remembered.

Though I was willing to answer his questions, I hadn't told him much about me. Why take the risk? Wasn't it too soon to be in love? Or was it different for men? I remembered a flirty girl from high school sitting next to me nearly fifty years ago. She was talking to her friend. "I'm not in love, but I think I'm in serious like." She nailed it, and I hung on to her words, because I didn't know what loving a man would feel like. This was a perfect description of how I felt about Richard. Maybe passion would come in time.

* * *

Four more emails came from him that day, and the next day brought an additional four. I was both intrigued and overwhelmed.

Also flattered.

How I hoped that my fears were nothing more than mild, congenital paranoia. My parents had taught me the importance of being cautious. If a boy took advantage, it would be my fault because of the way I dressed or because I wasn't acting like a lady or because I led him on. Their words still ran like a mantra, even though I first heard them in the Fifties. My parents warned me of things to watch out for long before I needed to know, though once an old man with cataracts had banged on the back door of our car on our way to swimming lessons, and if I had opened it, he might have snatched me.

Logically, there was nothing to fear from sex anymore. Richard would guide me, and there was no danger of pregnancy.

Later, while trying to read a magazine, my mind wandered again. I thought about practical things. What if he expected me to pay his bills? So many lonely women my age lost their life savings to con men. That wasn't me. Or him. I'd always managed my money and I wasn't going to turn that job over to anyone. Besides, Richard was too direct to be a con man. He had too many ties in the community and his church survived on a shoestring budget.

He kept sending emails. I wasn't used to the intense attention.

My Dear:

Why is it that I spend so much time thinking about you when you are not with me? Why do I have such anticipation for our next meeting? Why? Why? Why? I suppose only the shadow knows.

Silly, I know. I responded anyway. A few hours later he wrote more.

I once met a woman-child

She was not like any other I have ever met.

She's sweet and kind, and wise as an owl but innocent as a bird,

She's eager to please, but does not know how,

She's happy and sad, maybe lonely, dedicated to others yet none have been there for her.

I think I would like to be there for her as none has been before, to laugh, to cry, to have and to hold, to bring joy to her soul.

I'm not a child, I thought as I walked Mikko in the park by my condo. Never having crossed the traditional threshold into womanhood was not a limitation except when a man expected more than I knew how to give. I had assumed all the public responsibilities of a grown woman, but I had never experienced intimacy.

"Were you ever a daddy, Little Mikko? What was it like?"

Ridiculous seeking help from a dog. Like Richard, though, Mikko never judged me. Unlike Richard, he didn't answer.

Maybe our different lifestyles and levels of education didn't matter. I didn't want to give up having this man in my life. Besides, maybe he found what he wanted and wasn't willing to let me slip away. I wrote him about my fears, and he sent me another email.

Life is so wonderful, so full of mystery and the fear of the unknown. You think you know what you want but you fear the unknown . . .

I still accept the challenge and the unknown and though I fear the unknown, I eagerly await it.

Anyone who eagerly awaited the unknown, even though he feared it, was more courageous than I was. Why accept a challenge that I hadn't issued? Was he taking poetic license? Or was love an obsession, especially in the early stages?

He was certainly letting vulnerable parts of himself appear, and I could not remember any man ever doing that before.

The next weekend we went out to dinner at an Italian restaurant. He offered to see one of the movies chosen by the film group I was in—the one that kept me from meeting him that Friday night and moved our first date up to that Thursday. Apparently, he was falling for me much faster than I was falling for him. Meanwhile, I basked in wonder and disbelief.

> *Life is full of mystery's and joy. I'm looking forward to the journey we have started and to where it will go. The sky is the limit and the only thing we have to fear is fear itself. I'm willing to take the chance, how about you?*
>
> *I LOVE YOU!*
>
> *Rich*

Looking forward to the journey? Absolutely.

I couldn't call him Rich, though. One of the most manipulative liars I'd ever known was a high school student named Rich. He lied about homework, cheated on tests, forged his mom's signature, and disrespected me to win approval from his classmates. Rich, the student, was the opposite of my Richard, and I wasn't about to let him go because of a shortened name.

If I were keeping score, that would have been a point for love. I couldn't help wondering if the universe was trying to warn me to be careful about this man, who was falling in love so much more quickly than I could. That was a point for caution. If love was a game, the score was tied.

CHAPTER 8

ONE HOT AUGUST night, my kitchen window was open, and the neighbors could probably hear me screaming, "I've got to get out of this!" Maybe half of Danville could hear. I didn't care.

I worked myself into a frenzy on the forty-minute trip back from Bible study. Because the days were getting shorter, long shadows took over the roadway. Though I realized I'd soon be driving this in the dark, what really upset me was my ignorance about people. How could I stay in this relationship without losing myself in his world? On the other hand, was there a way to leave without turning my life back into the big, empty zero it had been in the year since Warren died?

When Richard came into my life, I received massive attention. The most loving man I'd ever met was also the most controlling. Maybe Richard was too honest for me. He spoke freely about his past, his mistakes, his successes, his beliefs, and his needs. He didn't hedge. Every time he told me that he had to be the head of the household because it was the Biblical way, the good feeling inside me curdled.

Was he testing me? His first wife used to say, "Behind every good man is a woman, standing there with her arms crossed, rolling her eyes." When he told me that, he laughed. So, this head-of-the-household thing was an impossible dream and he knew it. He considered himself the decision maker because that was the role he expected to play. Most of the time, I humored him. I wasn't about to defer to him because he was the man. No way.

More and more, I wondered if he talked about male superiority just to get a reaction. If I blew up, I proved that women were emotional. If I said nothing, I was being passive and asking to be led. This ridiculousness was enough to make any sane woman scream, "I have to get out." I tried it in my car.

And it happened again the minute I got home. Tremendously distressed, I slammed the front door, headed straight for the refrigerator and screamed, "I have to get out!"

Sometimes Richard frustrated me and he didn't know that he was doing it. Rather than end our relationship, I wanted him to admit that we had separate but equal talents. I provided the Goodwin Spelling Service whenever he typed a word with a squiggly line underneath, and he put in GFIs and installed LED overhead lights.

Unlike him, I didn't take every word of the Old Testament literally, and I believed that God didn't expect me to. Combining history and culture, the Old Testament was a depiction of life in the Middle East two thousand years ago. Today, women could and should be equal partners with men in anything that did not require upper body strength.

"I can't do this," I shouted again, grabbing handfuls of hair because it was better than ramming my head into the refrigerator. "I can't let him siphon off my independence." Maybe yanking against my scalp would divert my rage.

Richard owned his mistakes. I hid mine—especially when I felt like I was losing it, as I did at that moment. As long as I didn't pull out clumps of hair, I could deny the whole explosion. The neighbors had heard me scream before. Besides, the condos on either side of me were dark.

So, when I saw Richard coming up the walk as "I have to get out of this" came out of my mouth, I froze. I couldn't hit rewind or erase. I couldn't deny those words. If he came in and said *you're acting just like a woman*, how would I defend myself?

Though part of me was crying out *no! I don't mean it*, I refused to give him the upper hand. Even though he had an incredibly steady temper, he couldn't throw his superiority at me unless I let him. He couldn't be the head of the household when this place had been mine for over thirty years.

"Is this it?" Richard asked in an annoyingly neutral voice as he walked into the kitchen.

"No. I wouldn't blame you if you wanted to leave, though."

He stepped forward and put his arms around me. I backed into the kitchen counter.

"I'm not going to leave. I'm in this for the long haul." He meant it kindly. He wasn't shouting, blaming, or accusing. He was trying to calm me down. How my resentment grew. The last thing I wanted was anybody touching me when I was in a boiling rage. Why couldn't Mr. Self-Control let me have my feelings?

No wonder I kept screaming when I didn't really mean it. How had I given control of my life to a man I met less than two months ago on Craigslist?

"I wasn't talking about you," I said to my shoes. Idiotic and illogical? Yes. However, I did not want to hurt him. He was the best thing that ever happened to me. We had fun together, and in a few short weeks I had stopped trying to impress him or change myself for him. Most of the time, he made me comfortable. He valued my intelligence and sense of humor.

I refused to become his dependent. Nor would I bankroll his projects. But even though I wanted to be left alone, I didn't want him to leave. Too confusing. Was I more afraid of Richard or loneliness?

All I wanted was to wipe out the last few minutes, and I couldn't do that.

Why couldn't I say, *I'm just overwhelmed and don't want to talk about it? Do you want me to fix you some coffee?* Even that wouldn't have been right. I didn't want to make him coffee. My most important task was to help him forget my outburst.

Wasn't there a way to be with him and not lose myself in his world?

* * *

The next night over dinner, Richard said, "Our lives are like a Venn diagram. Do you know what that is?"

"It's when two circles overlap because they have something in common, isn't it?"

"How did you know that?" he asked.

"Two search words are better than one."

He looked puzzled.

"Fifteen years ago, a library computer specialist held up a sample of a Venn diagram in a staff class about searching Google. She wanted to show us why two search words were better than one."

"Tell me more."

After telling him about the class I asked, "Why do you think we're like a Venn diagram?"

"I figure we're different in so many ways, and yet we have areas in common."

True. We were both in our sixties and lonely enough to use Craigslist to find a companion. In addition, we were both willing to talk and good at figuring things out. He would probably add that we were both Christians, though I would counter that we had different ways of practicing our faith. Better not go there. We both liked adventures and eating out and movies, though I preferred dramas and he was hooked on action-adventures.

Neither of us assumed that we should be able to read each other's minds. Neither obsessed about sports. We both cooked, though he preferred salt, grease, and beef to salads, pastas, and veggies. Neither of us was obsessed with either our physical appearances or household cleanliness, though neither one of us was a complete slob. We both resisted the boredom of total retirement. Both of us believed in God.

Our differences were more extensive. He was totally honest and said whatever he thought. I hid my feelings and blew up without warning. He stayed calm, despite the pressures of work and church. He was pain-free and had to control his diabetes daily. I had no diabetes but was on daily medication to control the pain of fibromyalgia.

Other differences crept in as I looked at our backgrounds. He was born in San Antonio, Texas, and I was born in San Jose, California. He grew up in Corpus Christi, and I grew up in Los Gatos. In high school, I was expected to earn at least three As and a B in academic subjects. It was a rule in our family. If you didn't make those grades, you were grounded for the next quarter. Richard skated by with Cs, and never cracked a book. His dad told him that he wasn't smart enough to be a lawyer, and Richard took up a trade rather than a profession.

His biological father was shot down over Saipan in July 1944, and he was born in September of that year. I lost my emotionally distant dad when I was thirty-two. Richard still had the only dad he ever knew, who was technically his stepfather. Both of us had mothers who survived our fathers and moved on with their lives.

Despite our differences, there was something about him that overrode every external consideration. I felt safe with him and trusted him because he hid nothing.

He married a sixteen-year-old high school junior when he was twenty. They stayed married for forty years until she collapsed and passed away. She had been through cancer. They accepted that she didn't have much time left, and were traveling to Arkansas so she could visit her relatives one last time. They didn't even make it out of

California. She died in their RV outside Bakersfield. Jean always told Richard, "When I die, you'll be married within a month." He showed her, though. He waited six weeks. They both agreed he wouldn't be happy alone.

He married one of her caregivers. His new wife, Joan, had a pacemaker. He didn't care. He had a partner. I didn't believe he could fall in love that fast, and when I eventually asked, he told me that their love grew over time. Joan died the day after their third anniversary, and Richard was, again, by himself.

So, our Venn diagram didn't cross over in many places. Richard was an electrical contractor and pastor. I was a writer, teacher, and editor. He had an associate degree in applied science in electronic technology from Del Mar College. I held a bachelor of arts in drama from Vassar, a master's degree from San Francisco State University, and lapsed high school and community college teaching credentials. I wasn't used to sharing. He fell into it naturally. I saved part of almost every paycheck I ever earned. With a wife and seven kids to support, he saved nothing.

I never believed that opposites were attracted to one another until I met Richard. Part of the allure was that we got along so well despite our differences. Part of the fear was that I was on a pink cloud.

He wanted to marry me as soon as possible. I wanted to wait. He said he needed the influence of a good woman. I avoided the restrictions imposed by any man. Partners in a marriage are supposed to be equal—different in their skills and attributes but equal in the way they view each other and the way the world treats them.

People treated me differently in restaurants and campgrounds when I was with Richard. Waitresses looked at me knowingly as Richard ordered our food, and we developed a camaraderie. Men held doors open for me. Questions swirled. Was I presenting myself more confidently in the world? Was this one of the perks of being half a couple? Was I smiling more? Had my posture changed?

Eventually, I realized that they treated me better even if I wasn't with him. Being his woman affected the way I interacted with the world. Ushers smiled when they told me what theater the movie was in. Church members talked to me about their kids, their budget, and the way the world was treating them, as if I had something important to say. Even the local grocery clerks were friendlier.

Richard met my needs for appreciation about ninety-five percent of the time. Whenever I asked about his day, he told me about the checks that came in and the supplies he needed and the jobs he was bidding. He told me about church issues and asked my opinion. He didn't ask me about my day on a regular basis. Sometimes I volunteered. Sometimes I stayed silent. My talk of clients or characters was as foreign to him as amps, ohms, and tools were to me. We did not have a common work vocabulary.

Once we talked about our days, and said *uh huh* to each other a dozen times without really understanding, we stopped talking and kissed instead.

CHAPTER 9

AS WE SAT across from each other at a diner, Richard said, "I love you." He told me once that it was important to say those words aloud. Repetition was reinforcement. Hearing him say that he loved me did matter, although it bothered me that he said the words without thinking.

"I love you, too," I answered. No passion. Just words said on autopilot. Even though I made eye contact, there was more compliance than love in my tone. Compliance is not love.

Did he notice? Was I finding fault with him again?

When would I trust Richard's motives and accept him?

No book could answer my questions or remove my doubts. We were moving forward way too fast for me—not for him. Even after my blow-up in the kitchen, I still met his expectations. At least that's what he said. As far as I knew, he held nothing back. Then again, a niggling voice warned me not to be so naïve.

We both believed it was no accident that I went into Craigslist right after he reposted his ad. His Fourth of July church campout with the Russian lady as his date had been a disaster, and my Fourth of July alone watching the families in Danville was nearly as bad. I wanted to date, to make up for lost time, to fill my life with experiences and restaurants and day trips. Did I love him enough for marriage? Not yet. But why not give love a chance to grow?

That was what happened with his second wife, Joan, though it happened after they exchanged wedding rings. He liked more than loved her when he lost Jean, and was intensely lonely. Joan, who was a caregiver, had no place to go after Jean died. According to Richard's beliefs, it wouldn't be right for Joan to keep living in his house without the benefits of marriage. So six weeks after Jean passed away, he asked Joan to marry him. Joan jumped at the chance. He believed that they would fall more deeply in love and they did. Richard could make that happen.

As he tells it, they had a blast, going places and doing anything she had enough breath for. She had an enlarged heart and had to be careful about her activities. If she could climb a flight of steps, she was healthy enough to make love, the doctor had said. And that was the rule that guided them. She died three years and one day after their wedding.

Although he dated again, nothing came of it. He was getting older. So was I by the time we met. We shared an unspoken worry: *Is this my last chance?*

* * *

At the September meeting of my *Sun Magazine* group, we hung out in a Danville kitchen, assembling our monthly potluck dinner. As the women stood around the island in the kitchen, mixing salads and putting out appetizers, I told them about Richard.

Heads turned. Eyes widened. What happened to the quiet, asexual Lynn? After they got past the initial shock that I had a boyfriend, the group had questions.

"How old is he?" a woman who was still seeking her true love asked.

"Sixty-six."

The soon-to-be-divorced mother of a high school and college student asked, "How many kids does he have?"

"He and his first wife were going for an even half-dozen, but the last two were twins, so they have seven," I said. "All adults and out of the house. Several have children of their own."

She went on making her salad.

"So, what did he do for a living?" a woman who was job hunting asked.

"Does—not did. He's an electrical contractor, and on Sundays he pastors a small church." The pride in my voice surprised even me.

"Why is he still working?" she continued.

"He loves his jobs and loves being in charge. Besides, he doesn't feel like he has enough Social Security to retire on."

"Well, where did you meet him?"

"Craigslist." I said it deadpan.

Shock registered on every face. One woman gasped. Another said, "Are you kidding?" They wanted to protect me, just like the women in my free writing group and the women in my book club.

"I know how improbable it sounds, but he's not like anyone I've ever met."

"Look at her," the woman mixing the salad said. "She's falling hard."

When I described the ad in which he compared himself to a 1944 Roadster, they barely acknowledged the cleverness in his extended metaphor because Craigslist was an immediate red flag to them. Even though he'd been honest about his kids, about being a two-time widower, about his financial situation, and about his need for a wife, Craigslist was where women hooked up and sometimes ended up dead.

"Have you seen his place?" another woman asked.

"Sure." I wasn't about to tell them that he lived in a trailer to save money while he was between wives. Why fuel their judgment?

They warned me that this relationship could easily turn into a disaster. That was probably the crux of my fears. When I heard them say it, a defiant, stubborn streak flared up. These women misunderstood. Instead of asking for their approval, I was informing them. Richard's approval was all I needed.

In the same moment, he could make me giggle like a little girl and feel like his special woman. Dating was the first step. We were connecting the building blocks for a relationship. We hadn't met each other's families or talked about what they needed from us. Nor had we discussed retirement, just in case he ever decided to leave his job or I stopped writing. It was way too soon to know about forever.

As soon as he read my book about journaling, a very quick read, he spilled his thoughts on paper. It was still July when he sent me this description of love:

> *Love is:*
>
> *The Feeling You Get when the one you are attracted to gets near . . .*
>
> *The knowing that they feel the same way about you . . .*
>
> *The knowledge that they know your most intimate secrets and love you in spite of it . . .*
>
> *The joy of not being alone anymore . . .*
>
> *The joy of walking hand in hand . . .*
>
> *The intimate time we share together . . .*
>
> *The rough times we weather and work through as one . . .*
>
> *The fear of the unknown and the joy of facing it whenever . . .*
>
> *Yes, love is all of these and I long for this one again!*

It was wonderful journaling and a good definition. I took it apart, piece-by-piece. I was struck by his statement: "They know your most intimate secrets and love you in spite of it." Mark Twain once said something similar. We weathered my kitchen blow-up. That was a shameful secret more than an intimate one. What if he was just trying to fill the wife slot? Would any compliant, Christian woman do? If so, how could he not see the gap between who I was and who he wanted me to be?

* * *

One Saturday in September, we drove across the San Joaquin Valley farmlands, where the harvesting machines made a soothing drone as they gathered the crops. Heading into the foothills, pines towered over us. I was grateful for the shade. Sunlight saturated my skin as we crossed the valley. By the time we arrived in Yosemite, we were ready for the shade of cliffs that were so tall that they blocked the mid-afternoon sunlight.

We both got out of the car and shot photos of the steep cliffs scraping the sky and the late summer waterfalls trickling down. Richard used his Canon Rebel. I used my cell phone. While I was taking a quick candid of Richard with the camera at his eye, we heard two men shouting in a foreign language. Simultaneously, we turned and saw one lunging at the other on the far side of the parking lot. Their friends struggled to keep them apart.

"Get in the car and stay there," he commanded. I didn't argue. As soon as I was in, he headed across the lot to see if he could help. Sure, he was a pastor. *So what?* I didn't want him mixing it up with these dark-haired twenty-somethings screaming in a language we didn't recognize. What if one of them had a knife or a gun?

He was back in three minutes. He slid into the driver's seat, shoved the key in the ignition, and said, "Let's go." In the mirror on the passenger's side, I saw the park police.

"Be careful backing up," I murmured as he threw the gearshift into reverse.

The shouts came louder and faster as he swung around. A uniformed park ranger guarded the parking lot entrance. He put out a hand and Richard pulled the car to a stop. I pressed my lips together.

"Nobody can get in or out for a few minutes," the ranger said. "Did either of you see or hear anything?"

"We just came in to take pictures," Richard said as I shook my head. Maybe I watched too many movies, but I wondered if something illegal preceded the shouting. Uniforms and badges made me worry that the situation could flip out of control at a moment's notice.

We sat silently while the park police officer spoke to someone through the little black box on his shoulder. A moment later he waved us through. We never found out what happened, or why they let us go so quickly. Maybe the police saw us as an elderly couple, married many years, and wanted us out of the way so we wouldn't get hurt. One more reason I liked being with Richard.

Standing in the shade of the redwoods later, Richard suggested that we go on the Valley Floor Tour to hear the history of the giant trees. He bought our tickets, and while we were waiting, a young couple giggled as they tried to get into a selfie.

Richard said, "Would you like me to take a picture of you and your girlfriend?"

Delighted by his generosity, the man explained which buttons to push, while his girlfriend and I watched. Then the dark-haired man put his arm around the girl, I ducked out of the way, and they both smiled.

"Look at each other," Richard suggested after he took a couple of shots. They laughed and followed his directions while he snapped more photos.

"Fabulous," the young brunette said when she looked at the results. "Thank you so much."

Though he was always generous, today he had an ulterior motive. "Now would you take our picture?" he asked. He showed the man how to click and zoom on his camera. Then he put his arm around me and we posed in front of a giant redwood. Afterwards, when we looked into the monitor, I saw Richard in his pale purple, button-down shirt and me in my blue-flower tee. I was about his size, and we were both comfortable with that.

What surprised me was the joy in my eyes and the excited smile on my face. Never before had I looked that way in a photo—not even a graduation picture. I was a woman in love with life, a byproduct of being in love with Richard. Even though we weren't looking at each other, the picture broadcast the strong connection between us. It was physical evidence of what I had not been able to feel. Just as he predicted in July, he made me fall in love with him. My doubts never discouraged him. Summer 2011 had turned into the best summer of my life, and I had to look at a snapshot to see it.

Love crept in without my even recognizing it. "Beautiful. Send me the picture," I said. That night, I made it my new Facebook profile picture. I waited for people to write back and say, "Who is that man and how did you meet him?"

The answer to the first question was easy. The answer to the second one embarrassed me. Even though Richard was a gem, it was hard to admit that we met on Craigslist.

CHAPTER 10

LATER IN SEPTEMBER, Richard decided that it was time to introduce me to his dad, his siblings and their families. All of them lived in Texas.

In July he'd asked to see where I grew up, and we drove past my first home in Campbell, where the fence that I once scrambled up now only reached my knees. After that, I took him to my second home in Los Gatos, where my parents' bedroom windows looked out over Santa Clara Valley, before it was Silicon Valley.

As we planned our trip to Texas, I realized this was additional proof that he considered me more than a Craigslist bargain. He was serious about our relationship because he considered me *The One*. When a book club friend pointed out that his attention put me in the driver's seat of this relationship, my confidence swelled. How I liked discovering that hidden power.

On the morning we left, he asked, "Do you have the tickets?" as he loaded our bags into the trunk of my Camry.

"Yes," I said, patting my giant purse. "Do you have your cell phone and your blue tooth?"

He patted his pocket.

The previous night I warned him that I often teared up when a plane took off.

"No worries," he said.

"A seatmate told me years ago that it's a release of nervous tension."

"I love you," was all he said. Once again, he accepted me as is.

My teary reaction started on the first flight I took after my mother died. I hadn't been on a plane in six years. Once she was gone, everything shifted. Tears flooded my eyes as the plane accelerated on the runway and lifted into the air. I was having the same sensation of leaving earth that she experienced on the day she passed away. Did her soul cruise down a runway and pick up speed before it lifted off and separated from her body? I never considered death being like a liftoff until that moment. I was probably still grieving. Now, though, I was busy living.

As Richard pulled out of the driveway I asked, "Should we take Highway 24 or 580?"

"Highway 24's better."

"Maybe, as long as we don't get caught at the tunnel or the bridge. David used to take 580 from here, and he drove professionally. So, he should know." I'd only seen my activities group friend once since I started dating Richard.

"Let's give it a try," Richard said. It was an auspicious beginning for the trip.

Forty minutes later, we were driving down Doolittle towards the Oakland Airport when he suddenly exclaimed, "I don't believe it." His usual calm manner was gone. He reached under the seat. He checked the console. He touched his pocket.

"What?"

"I left my wallet in my car."

He often left his wallet in his car. Usually it happened when we went out to dinner. I always told myself that it was not a big deal.

I could afford to treat. "I can lend you some money." I had plenty if we used my charge cards.

"I can't get on the plane without my driver's license."

Or drive a rental car, I thought as he made a sharp U-turn. He accelerated. I shrank into my seat and breathed so softly that he could not hear. Of course he was angry. And probably frustrated and embarrassed. If I were in his position, I would be too. No one wants to be disorganized on a trip to see his family, much less when he's trying to show his prospective wife what a good head of the household he would be.

"If we miss the flight, we can reschedule for tomorrow," I said as we barreled down the freeway.

He didn't answer. Maybe he didn't hear me. By the time we got back to my garage, my knees and thighs ached from pressing into each other since we swung around on Ninety-Eighth Avenue. I reached up and pushed the button for the garage door while he threw open the driver's door and raced out. He didn't even stop to turn off the engine or put on the emergency brake. He reached into the Mazda and grabbed his well-worn wallet. When he held up his right hand, I called out, "Victory!"

Punching the button to close the garage door while we sped away, he said, "Thirty-five minutes. We can still make it." How I hoped he was right.

We pulled our luggage out of the trunk. Richard took one suitcase in each hand, running for the bus with me loping lopsidedly after him. I favored my right leg and clutched my purse against my stomach. Richard hoisted both suitcases onto the bus while I pulled myself up with the help of the metal poles on the steps. He plopped down beside me.

I took his hand and said, "We'll make it." He checked his watch and nodded.

As we rode toward the terminal, I handed him the tickets. "Run. Tell them I'm on my way." My heart pounded. "Tell 'em I'm disabled."

I might be by the time I made it to the gate. "Make 'em wait for me."

The bus let us off at Terminal Two. Inside, we faced long lines at security. We removed our shoes. We inched forward. I calmed my gasping breath as we advanced and waited. He dumped the contents of his jacket and pants pockets into a bowl. I dropped my purse in the next plastic container.

"Laptops," Richard said. I pulled mine out and placed it on top of my purse. He put his underneath his jacket. Stepping into the security screening first, he cleared it in less than thirty seconds. Then it was my turn. Raising my arms, I hoped my underwire didn't set off an alarm. An attendant did a slow body scan with her wand before she let me go. Richard already had his shoes and jacket on when I was still tying my shoes.

"Go! Make them wait."

He wouldn't leave me. After stuffing my laptop in the front compartment, I grabbed my suitcase and threw my jacket over my purse. He took both suitcases again and we jogged towards the escalators. On the second floor, I started gasping.

"Final boarding call for Flight 47."

"Go," I insisted. "Make them hold the plane."

There was no other choice. No way we were missing the plane.

I limped my way through the terminal with as much energy as I could muster. Richard looked back to make sure I hadn't fallen. I nodded. I raced to the gate, gasping, and the attendant handed me my boarding pass. "Go," she said. "They're closing the door in one minute."

We rushed down the ramp, over the threshold, and into the cabin. Miraculously, we found two seats together. With no space in the overhead bin for our suitcases, Richard searched for spots elsewhere. I slid into the middle seat and fastened my seatbelt, trying to slow my breathing.

As the plane taxied down the runway, Richard took my hand. Silently saying the Lord's Prayer, just in case, was good therapy.

Since that tearful flight eight years earlier, I'd entered a whole new world. This time I was flying halfway across the country with my—gulp—boyfriend. No boy or man, not even Warren, had ever taken me to meet his family before, and Warren's family lived in the same county. Maybe my excitement cured my fear of flying. Maybe Richard's love had. We were on an adventure. Better late than never.

After forty-five minutes in the air, I was concentrating on a novel when Richard grabbed my arm and said, "I think I left my laptop at the gate."

"You didn't put it back in your suitcase?"

He shook his head. "Don't know."

"Go check. If it's not there, maybe someone can call the gate from the plane."

Please, God, protect his laptop and let him find it in the suitcase, if that is Your will, I said silently. Standing halfway up the aisle, Richard pulled the suitcase out of the overhead. When he set it on the floor, he was out of my sight. As he returned the suitcase to the overhead compartment, he didn't look at me. Instead he talked to the flight attendant.

"They can't call the gate from the plane," he said as he sat down two minutes later.

"Call the airport as soon as we land," I suggested.

"No phone number."

"You're not the first person to leave something behind. Ask the flight attendant what to do."

When he came back, he was holding a cup of coffee, which meant that things were improving. "She suggested the same thing and gave me the number for the Oakland Airport." He opened his book, and lifted the post-it that marked the place where he stopped reading. I was impressed. This was beyond his control and he refused to let it eat away at him.

Once we were inside the Houston terminal, he called Oakland and explained the situation. His face remained neutral as the person on the other end spoke.

I stared at the ground and at the backs of our fellow passengers bustling down the hall. He tucked his phone back in his pocket and said, "Anything left behind is taken to Lost and Found. It should be there when we get back. We go to the second floor, Room 201."

He could use his phone for email. Everything else would have to wait. There was no alternative. Maybe this was a secret blessing. No work on this trip.

Richard had an uncanny ability to let go of the things he couldn't control. That was one of the things I loved about him, and I hoped that wouldn't change, no matter what stressors came up while we were in Texas.

CHAPTER 11

ONCE WE LANDED at Houston Hobby Airport, I was happy to let Richard carry the bags. He reset his GPS to Texas and drove the rental car out of the Avis parking lot. We were in his territory now, not mine.

Once we left Houston, I couldn't take my eyes off the low-lying bushes, dotted with ripe cotton, that filled the vast, flat land. The sky, a boundless blue dome, set the stage.

"Are you hungry?" he asked when we were still about an hour away from his sister's place in Needville.

"If you are."

"Does this look good?" he asked as he swung into the parking lot of an authentic-looking Tex-Mex restaurant.

"Fine with me." Although we gained two hours with the flight, my body dragged. Probably a fibromyalgia reaction to racing through the airport.

We had just been escorted to a booth in the dimly lit restaurant when his phone rang. Business continued, even when we were away. There was nothing for me to do but wait, unless I took out my book and read. I didn't want to be rude. I could see the distress etched on his face. I wanted to help but had no idea how to solve his business problems. A creeping fear that he might see me differently once he was with his family took hold.

The phone call continued, so I slid out my book and held it on my lap. It was hard to read that way. Reviewing books was part of my job, just as long-distance trouble-shooting was part of his. Of course, our jobs weren't equal. He signed contracts for huge sums of money in order to cover wages, parts, and business expenses every week. Still, it made sense for me to pursue my work while he was on the phone with his. As soon as he put away his phone, I would close my book.

Once he was done, he asked, "What should we order?"

"I'll take a chicken enchilada and rice. The rest is up to you." That was my standard answer in any Mexican restaurant.

Another call came in. I reopened my book. Sure enough, he ordered our traditional three-item combo between phone calls.

When the food arrived, Richard insisted that what we got was not even on the menu. The waiter showed him, and they disagreed about what the words meant. The waiter, with a heavy Hispanic accent, left to check with the kitchen. A few minutes later he returned and said that we were the ones who misunderstood. It wasn't good customer relations, and I understood why Richard was upset, but usually he was much more forgiving.

Was he more bothered by the laptop than I realized? Or the trip back to Danville to pick up his wallet? Or the whole morning? Maybe I didn't know him as well as I thought.

We ate quietly, skipped desert, and by the time we were back on the road, his anger defused. I couldn't read his mind. He seemed okay with everything as we continued past crops and occasional farm and ranch houses. Driving relaxed him more than being a passenger calmed me.

At last, he turned onto a long dirt driveway.

"That's the place," he said, with warmth and pride in his voice.

I looked out on the immense acreage. An empty pond and a wooden dock with two Adirondack chairs sat right in the middle of all that blowing grass. A tall windmill with wooden paddles that didn't turn stood next to the dock.

"We used to swim in there," he said as we drove past.

We parked in front of a two-story house with gables. I was about to get out when a slender, white-haired woman carrying a covered dish walked up to the driver's side.

"Marsha, good to see you." There was a boyish excitement in Richard's voice as he added, "This is Lynn."

Marsha was the older sister I had heard so many fabulous stories about. She was dressed casually, in jeans and a dark top. She welcomed me with warm eyes, a big smile, and the elongated vowels of her Texas drawl. The two of them chatted for a minute while I drank in the sultry air.

His younger sister, Debbie, was filling water glasses when we walked into her kitchen. Her eyes lit up when she saw her brother. "You look great," she told him.

He turned towards me and beamed as he said, "This is Lynn."

Debbie took us down the darkened hall, lined with Marsha's photographs of the family. Debbie had three daughters, including identical twins, Hailey and Hannah. In one shot of them on the weight-lifting team, they looked like mirror images wearing different numbers on their tops. They literally looked like clones, and Marsha's photography skills enhanced that. Even more, they looked comfortable being twins. Richard had two sons who were also were twins. Sam and David didn't look or act alike. Hailey and Hannah looked like they thrived on their similarities.

Debbie opened the door to a small room at the end of the hall. A double bed, a child-size desk, and an armoire filled most of it.

"This is Heather's room," Debbie said. "She's spending the night with a friend, so you'll be staying here." Heather was her eldest.

The minute we set down our suitcases, Richard was eager for me to meet his father, who lived in a luxury RV parked inside the barn closest to the house. As soon as we walked in, my understanding of barns changed. This one was clean, cavernous, and cool. The space contained lots of woodworking equipment and no trace of animals.

Richard knocked on the exterior door of a spotless trailer, and his father, Bill Huffman, called out, "Come in." He was a gentle, elderly man with age spots, glasses sitting crookedly on his face, and a kind smile.

While Richard and his dad reminisced, I sat at his polished oak desk. Bill never used the computer on it. He didn't even have email—just like my mom, who had been gone for a decade. I tried to imagine whether she would be pleased or shocked that I was sitting in this trailer, listening to my boyfriend and his father talk.

A moment later, I turned my attention back to Richard and his dad. I loved the joy in both of their faces as they shared stories about the past and the huge family. How I loved imagining Richard's past.

By the time we returned to the house, I'd hit a wall. That's how we described the times when fibromyalgia caught up and I had to stop. I lay down on Heather's bed to rest for a couple minutes. The next thing I knew, Richard was shaking my shoulder. It was suppertime.

Before they sat down to dinner, every member of the family would say something they were grateful for. Debbie and her family had wanted me to hear it, but by the time I sat down at the table, they'd already finished their ritual. I didn't get a chance to say that I was grateful to have Richard in my life. Of course, that also meant I didn't have to explain that we met on Craigslist. Probably they already knew. Maybe it was a blessing in disguise.

Debbie served an authentic Tex-Mex dinner, and Richard was in his element. Two Tex-Mex meals in one day. This time, he loved the food. I was also learning to enjoy mild Mexican dishes. Tonight, though, I was more interested in the company.

The twins joined us for supper. In addition to looking alike, they had identical-sounding, high-pitched voices. So similar. I'd never lived with twins, and I wondered if boyfriends might bring out their individual differences—especially if one married and the other one didn't. More and more, I observed how partners changed each other—sometimes for the better and sometimes not.

After dinner, Debbie's daughters put away the food and did the dishes, while Richard went outside for more conversation with Bill. The rest of us joined him, one by one.

The sun sank in a fireball, the sky darkened, and the stars appeared. I sat near the fire pit—not lit on this warm night—and listened while the family caught up on each other's lives. They welcomed me and allowed me to feel completely comfortable. Marsha had been a math teacher, and Debbie still taught middle school, so we compared notes on kids, schools, and parents' expectations.

We were on our way to bed when Richard reached into his suitcase for the bag containing his razor, hair gel, and pills. He dug deeper. He pulled out clothes. He stirred everything around, and a moment later he said, "I must have left my ditty bag in your trunk. We were in such a hurry."

Three items misplaced. I was used to keeping track of my stuff, and I figured he could take care of his.

Surely he knew how to pack. I was his girlfriend, not his mother. Sometimes a wife or a wife-to-be filled both roles—especially if her husband was overwhelmed. How I wished I had made sure he had everything before we left.

I decided every couple should have a checklist as we did in my family growing up. Back then, the list had three items: watch, rings, keys. Now it was more complicated. Cell phone, blue tooth (his), laptop, charger cords, pills, diabetes kit (his), and keys. I used my cell phone as my watch, and if I decided to get married, I planned to wear my ring all the time.

I reminded myself that it wasn't my bag. Nor was it my fault that we had to go back for his wallet. Or that he left his laptop in the airport. He wasn't imposing any guilt on me. I did that all by myself. Or maybe

I understood more about what it meant to be in a relationship. I saw why he needed a wife, even if he had his own routine.

"What do we do about your pills?" I asked, as we got ready for bed.

"I don't need them."

"Really?" Why do you take them if he doesn't need them? And what kind of diabetic doesn't need his medication?

"I'll be fine for a few days. I've gone without them before."

Sometimes I went without my pills, and within thirty-six hours the fibromyalgia symptoms kicked in and I was staggering around devoid of energy and hope. Our conditions were different, but our pills were prescribed because we each had medical needs.

At least I could call a hospital if I had to. I helped and supported him in every way I could. I refused, however, to hover. Especially in front of his family. I'd hate it if someone did that to me.

He was ready for bed and I was in the process of changing into my nightshirt when my foot slid awkwardly and unexpectedly. I lurched, grabbed a handful of air, and slammed my right knee and then my whole body into the tile floor. Flat on my face, I gasped for air. At least no scream came out of me this time.

I reached for the top of Heather's hope chest to pull myself up, and Richard said, "Sit for a minute."

"Good idea." My answer sounded light, even though I was shaking. The pain in my right knee burned, the nerve endings stung, and the last thing I wanted was an injury that would ruin this trip. Richard reached down and put his hands under my arms. Before, I was always alone when I fell. I didn't know if my muscles would cooperate or rebel if he pulled me up from my armpits.

"Ready?"

"I'm not sure."

"How do you want me to lift you?"

"Don't know." Putting my hands back on the wooden trunk at the foot of Heather's bed I said, "Spot me, okay?"

I tried to pull myself up. Nothing moved, so Richard slid his hands under my armpits as he had originally planned, lifted me and said, "You were overthinking it."

I was in fear. Bad enough that he pulled me up. He wasn't going to analyze my thought process. Besides, we were both right. I was on the floor, and I couldn't get back up. Moving my knee back and forth made it ache. I could feel the swelling. Thankfully, I could bend it a little. Sleep would heal it, along with the anti-inflammatory I took at night.

We got in bed, with Richard closer to the door, and he turned off the light. Heather's nightlight rotated tiny stars across the ceiling. We stared up at the stars for a minute, then simultaneously turned towards each other. A thundering crash resounded, and then we were on the floor, and so was the mattress.

"You okay?" we asked each other in unison. Once we realized that we were both fine, we started laughing. We shushed each other. The rest of the family was sleeping down the hall.

"What happened?" I asked in an exaggerated whisper.

Together we looked at the mattress and box spring, which lay half on the bed frame and half off. The slats had collapsed. They weren't broken, they just slid off the bed frame. Heather probably weighed eighty pounds, while the two of us together were over three hundred.

Richard repaired the bed single-handedly while I massaged my sore knee. When it was ready, I slipped in first, and we lay there without moving for the rest of the night.

The next morning, he was up before me, as usual. He told Debbie what happened while he poured his first cup of coffee, and added, "We weren't doing anything, I promise. The bed just collapsed."

When he came back to the room, he told me Debbie laughed and said, "The slats are a little short. I've been asking Mike to fix it for ages." Mike, her husband, took care of it that day. If only every problem could be solved that easily.

CHAPTER 12

RICHARD AND I both liked to snack, so Friday morning after Debbie and Mike left for work and the girls were at their classes, we drove around Needville in our rented Mercury until we found a small country store. Richard parked in the soft dust bordering a weathered porch. A sheet of corrugated metal hung over the deck, protecting it from the Gulf winds and hurricanes. Despite the protection, the paint had peeled from the signs advertising Coke and RC Cola.

"This looks like a good place," Richard said as he picked up his wallet from the car's side pocket. "Want to come?"

"Wouldn't miss it for the world." After grabbing a twenty out of my wallet, we stowed my purse in the trunk. As we climbed the worn wooden steps, a hollow *clomp* echoed as we crossed the old wood. A screen door sagged on its hinges, and two wooden chairs sat on either side of the doorway. Classic.

Inside, I stood by the candy display to make way for a man and woman. Both wore cowboy hats—hers white and his black. Both had carved leather belts with broad silver buckles. She was bleached-blond, with a faded blue shirt and a country-western purse that displayed a sequined cross on one side. The woman radiated brassy confidence and overshadowed the slender man who followed her. They could have been straight out of Central Casting.

I couldn't keep the smile off my face. I was really here. In the South. With a man who loved me. Everyone needed a slice of adventure. Finally, after sixty-two years, I found an amazing man who filled me with optimism. Unlike Warren, who never invited me to any family events, Richard was eager for me to get to know his dad and his siblings. I tingled with the promise of possibilities.

"Look what I found, honey."

I turned towards the refrigerator case, with its huge metal hinges and glass doors. Richard held up a twenty-ounce bottle of Big Red. The grin on his face reminded me of an eight-and-a-half-year-old with a lollipop. *Too cute.*

I kept thinking about the red dye and wondered how it might affect him. I wanted him healthy. However, I wasn't going to tell him to give up the soft drink he was so delighted to find. I hadn't even asked him to give up smoking, though he told everyone in the church, including me, "Smokers are a dying breed."

"I agree," I always said as he took another puff.

Friday and Saturday slipped away, and on Sunday morning, Richard wanted to show me the Intracoastal Waterway, which is a thirteen-hundred-mile, man-made canal that runs along the coastline bordering the Gulf of Mexico. Promising to be back for dinner, we told Debbie's family that we'd be exploring for most of the day.

They were ready to leave for church when I asked, "Do we lock the front door from the inside, or is there a key?"

Debbie and Mike burst out laughing. "If you locked it, we'd be in big trouble. Nobody knows where the key is anymore."

"It's different in the Bay Area," Richard explained.

There were still places where people don't lock their doors? I locked mine when I walked the dog. What a different world.

Within the hour, our stomachs rumbled. At a family restaurant where we stopped, the interior was straight out of a country-western ballad. When Richard asked the server if she was the owner, she practically snorted.

"Nope. I've always been a waitress, and that's all I'll ever be." Her crinkly, red lips smiled down at us. We tipped her well, wishing we could see her face when she saw it.

After breakfast, we headed for the beach. Hand in hand, we descended the cold, concrete steps, plowing through the sand until we got to that flat, damp place where sand and sea met. Listening to the waves and the gulls, we walked along the edge of the Gulf of Mexico. Gray clouds hung low in the sky, shielding us from the sun's intense rays.

As we headed toward the waves, the singles ads I read thirty years earlier popped into my head. Long walks on the beach were often mentioned. Even though I assumed that the words were written as a con job for some and a pipe dream for others, this walk gave me renewed hope. I'd buried my desires for long walks on the beach years ago. Though this was romantic, it was also damp and chilly. The thundering waves made it hard to hear.

When I shivered, Richard wrapped his arms around me. His kiss was long and slow. His tongue tickled mine until I was gasping and giggling.

"Ready to go back?" he asked.

I nodded. Walking across the sand was hard work. He kept me from slipping as we mounted the steps. Holding my feet outside the rental car, I wiped the sand with the commemorative beach towel we bought in a touristy store by the beach.

"Want to see more?" Richard pointed to a worm-shaped peninsula on the map. Together, we passed houses propped up on round, wooden beams driven deep into the sand. The Gulf of Mexico was a few feet away and the houses, with their tan, green, or pink paint and massive picture windows, contrasted with the Gulf's blue-green water. Gentle waves lapped against the shore. In a few months, the cars and boats parked under the houses would be swept away by hurricanes surging across the beach, unless they were stored somewhere else.

"Which one would you like to live in?" I asked Richard.

"I like that deck," he said, pointing to a wrap-around. "What about you?"

"Not sure if I could take the weather."

At lunchtime, we stopped at an outdoor café with open shutters and parakeet-green walls. The breeze from the Gulf blew through, ruffling our hair and making paper napkins fly. Palm trees swayed just beyond the shutters, their fronds rustling softly, reminding me of a restaurant at the edge of the Yucatan Peninsula, where I ate lunch six years earlier while on a tour with some Vassar alums.

Although the group visiting the Yucatan Peninsula was more intellectual and academic, Richard was more entertaining. He understood people and could put them at ease. I hoped some of his skills would rub off on me. Richard was already shifting my perspective. I liked being half of a couple instead of a single woman. While on the Yucatan Peninsula, I was just exploring. I was also filling time—something I no longer needed to do. On this adventure, I was filling in the blank spaces.

Richard returned from the trailer where they cooked our food. My enchilada and his taco and tamale filled a large plate, and he brought an extra plate so that we could split everything. He divided our food and said grace.

"Do you know why they cook in that trailer?" he asked as we ate.

"No idea."

"I asked the man why they were cooking outside, and he said it was so they could batten the trailer down and head for higher ground the minute there was a hurricane."

"Makes sense." But I could not see any higher ground. There was water on either side of the flat island. Maybe they hooked up their cooking area, threw their plastic chairs and tables and overhead tarps into a truck, and crossed the nearest bridge to the mainland. If that was the case, only the empty seating area would be battered by the storm.

Though I'd never seen a hurricane, I watched the reports of Katrina slamming into New Orleans in 2005. Louisiana was only one state to the east. The same hurricane probably hit the Intracoastal Waterway and shut down parts of Texas. Hurricanes were both dramatic and destructive. I was content watching them on TV. Adventures were fine, but there were limits. I hoped that Richard agreed.

After lunch, while he drove further east, I scanned the map looking for the easiest way to get back to the mainland. We were expected in Needville at six so that we could join the family at a seafood restaurant. Richard's father was treating his children and grandchildren. I found a route on our paper map. Richard's GPS, Cleo, disagreed. He called his sister, Debbie, and she confirmed that I was right. We women had to stick together. I stopped Cleo in her tracks. When I put in the address again, Cleo agreed to go my way. Loved it.

We stopped at his sister Marsha's house, and the two of them chatted about their memories of growing up in San Diego and Corpus Christi. The more I heard, the more I was amazed. Their memories meshed. Not always the case with siblings.

Thunderclouds loomed overhead, and before we arrived, fat raindrops splattered the car windows. It'd been sunny just a few hours earlier. Texas weather was dramatic. It was also new to me.

When we got to Joe's Crab Shack, Marsha got out first. She was standing under the awning, watching me struggle to straighten my legs and back. She looked scared and unsure of whether she should help.

"I have this trouble whenever it's wet," I said with the lightest voice I could muster. "Rain makes the pain worse, but your brother takes good care of me."

At that exact moment, I felt Richard's hand on my arm. In only a few months, he'd memorized my physical quirks. If I had to have fibromyalgia and arthritis, it was nice to have a supportive partner. He knew when to grab hold and when to let me rescue myself. If I was about to hit a wall of exhaustion, he saw the signs. When it was time for me to sit or get back into the car, he heard my small sighs. I was unaware of these hints. He would gently suggest that it was time to rest or sleep or take a pill. Despite my pride and stubbornness, he phrased his suggestions so that I cooperated without feeling manipulated.

When we arrived, the restaurant pushed six tables together for the Browns, Gibsons, Huffmans, and Hundls. The younger generation sat at one end while the rest of us picked chairs at the other end. I was close enough to the middle that I could hear both groups. The kids, who were actually college-age adults, talked about school, boyfriends, girlfriends, jobs, and plans for Heather's upcoming wedding. I loved the relaxed, happy nature of this family. I was fitting in for the first time in my life.

CHAPTER 13

I WAS SORRY to leave Texas. I loved the broad, bright skies and the casual friendliness of Richard's family. He made a leap of faith taking me there. If I compared him to his sisters and his dad, I might wonder why they had more money, given the fact that his dad gave to all of his children equally. In turn I worried that if his sisters compared me to his previous wives, I might not measure up. Paranoid? Yup. I preferred anticipating problems to having my expectations dashed.

When Richard told his dad that I was a saver, Bill said, "Well, good." When Richard told me about it, he added, "He was probably thinking it's about time."

Apparently, both his father and I loved Richard for who he was, and not for the impulsive choices he made. By the time we got on the plane for Oakland, I was ready to return to the familiar tasks of writing and reviewing, and even the increased grocery shopping and laundry that were now a part of my life.

Once we were off the plane, we stopped at Lost and Found.

Richard went in while I checked my phone and stared at the people greeting friends and family below. For once, the scenes of friends greeting friends didn't make me sad. When Richard came out of the Lost and Found with his laptop under his arm, I felt what he said so often: God is good.

* * *

The second night home, Richard and I were lying together. I was drifting off when I heard him ask, "If I were to ask you to marry me, would you accept Joan's ring?"

My throat tightened. I swallowed. It didn't help. Just when I was ready to get closer, he threw this into the mix. I wanted to ask him why he hadn't given the ring to Joan's daughter. After all, Jean's ring went to their oldest daughter.

Was I being selfish? Was I allowing him to walk all over me? Did he have any idea what a wedding ring meant? Scratch that one. Of course he knew. He'd been married twice before.

On the positive side, he told me who owed him money, what he collected, what he owed, and how much payroll was each week. The minute the checks came into his business, they were used. He had employees and suppliers to pay. He started his business without cash reserves, and for thirty-one years he treaded water, week after week, trusting God to provide.

I couldn't be responsible for his company's debts. We talked about that, too. Unlike Richard, I considered myself technically retired. I could work on any project—volunteered or paid—because I had a stash of savings, a bit of inheritance, a token retirement, and, in three more years, I'd collect a miniscule Social Security payment. All because I planned ahead, supported myself, and invested. I even contributed to Richard's personal needs. I just didn't have enough money to meet his weekly business bills.

The first time he said, "The secret to a good marriage is no secrets," I immediately said, "I would be uncomfortable telling you about my finances."

"Fine. We can keep that a secret as long as we both agree."

Being more financially stable, I agreed to share our living expenses. On our second date, when I offered to pay, he did say that I met one of his expectations. Over and over he promised that he did not want me for my money. Though I still believed him, I drew the line at accepting a used engagement ring. Unless it was a family heirloom. One could look at it either way. It was my choice.

Although I didn't want to be selfish, I couldn't accept his second wife's ring.

If he couldn't afford to buy a new one, how could he afford to marry me? This was the question a parent would ask a twenty-something, but I was sixty-two, with other questions. If I don't marry now, then when? I asked myself for the umpteenth time.

Back and forth, I weighed the pros and cons. Did he love me? Or did he just love having a wife? Men did have needs. And he was a Baptist pastor, who lived by doing the right thing. He could never stay with me without marriage. Though I wanted to stay in the relationship, I also wanted to be honest. Could I stall him?

Before I said anything else he added, "I want to marry you. But I can't afford a ring." He stared up at the darkened ceiling.

Hadn't I told him I wasn't ready? Did my opinion even matter?

"You know I won't be able to say *for richer or for poorer* in a wedding ceremony, right?" I said softly, stalling for time.

"I know. We've talked about that."

Richard had just asked me to marry him and now refused to look at me. Based on his tone, my reaction wasn't what he expected. Then again, the proposal wasn't the one I dreamed of either.

After a long, gaping silence, he added, "I'd buy you one of your own. I just don't have the money right now."

"I know," I whispered.

On the surface, our relationship didn't make sense. Friends and acquaintances wanted to know why I was drawn to him. And, at this particular moment, so did I. More and more I enjoyed the company of this man who said, "I love you." He took out the trash for me. Together, we visited the Russian River, Santa Cruz, Palm Desert, and Texas. And, most important, he made me laugh.

Spending time with him gave me purpose. So did his church. Now, on Sundays I wanted to participate. The church members' approval made me feel wanted and needed. The last time I experienced such acceptance, I was running the drama program at San Ramon High back when girls wore platform shoes and polyester clothes.

How would his second wife feel about my wearing her ring? A ring is a symbol of love. It represents commitment. When I married him, my ring could be a plain gold band and I'd wear it proudly. It would be proof that Richard had picked me.

Years earlier, my mother told me that she supplied the diamond for her engagement ring. After the divorce, she wore that diamond in a different setting, but it was still in a ring, and she wore it on the same finger until the day she passed away. Maybe there was more precedent for the man not buying a diamond than I realized. My rational side kept telling me that I was trying to convince myself that Richard's intentions were good.

What would my friends say if I wore a ring that belonged to his second wife? "One ring does not fit all." "Are you nuts?" I knew the answer. But why did it matter? My friends were not the issue. The nature of my relationship with Richard was what I really cared about.

Did Richard believe that wives were interchangeable?

Stop, Lynn. Just stop.

I was inventing worst-case scenarios. He wanted to marry me. Did I want to move forward or keep treading water?

"I love you," he said. In his next breath he was snoring.

In my wildest fantasies about marriage, I never imagined any man offering me his second wife's ring. I lay awake, staring at the ceiling as the lights from the park filtered through the mini-blinds.

The next morning, I thought about his offer. Instead of being indignant, I remembered our first kiss at the green fence that overlooked the ocean. Our first kiss in a movie theater, our first kiss on the beach in Galveston, and our first kiss on my doorstep. During that kiss, I pretended that we were a couple of high school seniors instead of real-life, pre-retirement seniors. Richard filled the holes in my life. He gave me the gift of a relationship. I didn't want to lose that any more than I wanted a used ring.

My fears spun around me. Whenever I tried to stop them, they popped back up, like a Bozo the Clown Bop Bag. The more they replayed, the less I knew who the Bozo was.

CHAPTER 14

THE NEXT NIGHT, Richard set a Mason jar on the dining room table. It was covered with a paper towel that was held in place by the metal lid of an old Skippy peanut butter jar. The price on the lid, stamped in purple ink, was forty-seven cents.

"Look inside." I found his childlike eagerness endearing, despite everything else.

Unscrewing the top, I lifted out a graduation ring. Next, I picked up a pin from the Boy Scouts, followed by a grade-school medal. Richard was sharing with me the highlights of his life in the jewelry that he saved. It was sweet.

A lady liberty silver dollar with cut-out segments giving a lacy effect hung on a tarnished silver chain. Minted in 1938. He wasn't born until 1944. I was too busy digging through the buried treasure to ask about its significance.

Inside this jar I also found an Indian-head penny, several twenty-five cent coins from the Pizza Time Theatre, a diez pesos coin from 1978, a liberty silver dollar from 1922, a pearl and gold necklace with a blank disc attached, a ruby-colored ring with a Masonic emblem, and a tiny gold cross on a child's gold bracelet. All of these trinkets painted a unique portrait of the man, to say the least. Almost at the bottom, I pulled out a paper towel. Inside was something round and flat.

"Take a look," he insisted.

From the paper towel, I pulled out a darkened gold band with a diamond in the center and little diamonds set in the channels on either side.

As I held it up to the light, Richard said, "Will you marry me?"

Much sweeter than the previous night. Even so, my stomach tightened. I waited a lifetime for this moment. I'd seen it played out in movies and read about it in books.

My mind refused to allow me to throw my arms around him and say *yes, oh yes, or what took you so long?* Again, I couldn't stop smiling. I wanted so much to say yes. But who was I kidding?

Staring at the ring, I asked, "Was this Joan's?"

"Yes," he replied.

Why was he always so honest? The eyes of an eager young boy shined through the laugh lines. It was hard to stay mad at him, even though he ignored my wishes. This was definitely not a storybook romance. I wanted him to take it from my hand and place it on my finger. Richard didn't move.

After staring at him for a few minutes, I said, "I think it will clean up nicely."

"I spent the afternoon soaking it in Polident."

"I thought the gold was tarnished. Maybe it's just my eyes." I slipped it on my finger, holding up my left hand. "The diamond's really sparkly."

"It looks nice," he said.

As if to confirm that we were now engaged, he leaned over and kissed me. I turned the word *nice* over and over in my head. Was that what a fiancé should say about the engagement ring he gives to his woman? I didn't love his choice of words. If I told him that I was uncomfortable, would he take his ring and go home? Or would he say, *take it off, I'm looking for a woman—not a girl*? On the other hand, he might say, *I understand*, giving me more time to think.

I stared at the ring that now adorned my finger. Already the diamond had rotated underneath. Were Joan's fingers even larger or more swollen than mine?

Then there were the practical things about life that we hadn't talked about. He loved his trailer. I loved my condo. His life was in the northwest corner of the county. Mine was in the southeast. I loved to read in the quiet. He liked books on tape.

"I want you to keep it," he said. "Even if you're not sure."

All I could do was smile. I was numb when I wanted to be joyous. Thank goodness, he never noticed. He had gotten his way. The ring was on my finger.

Wearing it to bed that night, I felt like a woman. The next morning it surprised me when it clunked against the refrigerator door and my coffee mug. I hadn't worn a ring on that finger since I was in the second grade. Unfortunately, every time the ring clanked against anything, I examined it to see if I damaged Joan's diamond. Joan's diamond. Not mine. Was I playing the role of an engaged woman, treating the ring like a costume? The woman in me was proud of the engagement. My stomach, however, quivered each time I looked at my hand.

The following morning, before I even opened my eyes, I felt for the metal band on my finger. Blinking and squinting, I opened my eyes to a sparkling diamond on a tarnished gold band. *Real or surreal?*

Once, we talked about Meg Ryan's fake orgasm when she was sitting in a café. I loved that movie—*When Harry Met Sally.*

"So that's what it's like?" I asked Richard as my grin got bigger and bigger.

"Absolutely," he replied, smiling.

After giving him my own fake orgasm sounds, I shook my

shoulders and rolled my eyes. Running my hands through my hair, I laughed. Imitation? Invitation? False advertising?

"I believe it," he said in a voice that could have been as fake as mine. I wasn't even sure.

That night, I cooked supper. Before we started to eat, he glanced down at my hand. I curled my fingers.

"You could have it resized, you know."

Staring at the ring, I filled the silence. "I know."

"What's wrong?"

Though I loved his directness, I couldn't reciprocate. Joan's ring felt like a foreign object on my finger. Instead, I replied, "Nothing."

"The secret to a good marriage is no secrets," he reminded me.

"We're not married."

"But we're going to be," he said.

And you're going to control my thoughts as well as my actions? I wanted to say. Unless I allowed it, he couldn't control me. How could I share my thoughts when they were hurtful to him?

"Tell me," he said. His request felt more like a command.

I shrugged. "I'm not used to it." When he didn't respond, I added, "It seems too soon to be engaged."

Again, he said nothing.

My heart refused to tell him that I never imagined that someday I would wear a previous wife's wedding ring. Or that I was afraid he wanted me for my money. What if he was waiting until we were married to tell me the truth?

"You're not ready to be engaged?" He sounded startled and angry. "Take it off."

I slid it off, held it between my thumb and forefinger, and handed it to him.

He shook his head. "You keep that. Put it on your dresser. Put it in that coaster where you keep your earrings."

My feet dragged against the carpet as I walked to the bedroom. With no tears, I was neither relieved nor upset. My lack of response puzzled me. I walked out feeling no connection to my emotions. I didn't want to say or do something that would end our relationship. But I needed more time. I had to be sure I was in love with him.

Why resist? Did I want something else that I was not even aware of?

Staring at the coaster that held the earrings, I held Joan's ring up to my lips and whispered, "Later."

Because I understood the reason Richard offered me a used wedding ring, I really wanted to accept it. There was just something that wasn't right. And I couldn't even name it.

Richard sat at the table sipping his coffee when I returned.

"Can I get you desert?" I asked.

Part servant. Part independent woman.

He ignored my question and said, "I want you to hold on to that ring until you're ready to wear it," his voice again gentle.

"Okay."

I never wanted to *have* to obey a husband. If a marriage couldn't be a full partnership, then I'd rather be independent and single.

"I'm sorry," I said. "I don't know what's wrong with me."

"You're fine. I love you. I want to marry you. And I've already told you that you don't lose until you quit trying. So, I'm not going to quit."

"I like your spirit, even though that's not always true. What about Hillary Clinton?"

"What about her?" he asked.

After losing the nomination in 2008, Hillary said she'd never run again. Although she became secretary of state, she couldn't control the opinions of the voters any more than she could control the behavior of her husband. She wanted to win an election. Hard as she tried, Hillary never achieved her goal.

"If she wants to be president badly enough, she can run again," Richard said.

His response in 2011 was without emotion or judgment. That was another thing I loved about him. He truly believed that you didn't lose until you quit trying. He never judged me. So I never had to defend my weight, my preoccupation with writing, or my empty history where a social life should have been. Richard accepted me as I was. Weren't men supposed to be the ones who were afraid of commitment? How had I let everything become so convoluted?

CHAPTER 15

NOT LONG AFTER I put the engagement ring away, Richard turned sixty-seven. We celebrated with a trip to the city to see the famous San Francisco musical, *Beach Blanket Babylon*. This unique farce is known for its extravagant hats and costumes, as well as its satiric political songs. For more than forty years, it had been playing at Club Fugazi on Green Street. We had both seen it before. The production company updated the songs and the costumes frequently. When Richard asked to see the latest version for his birthday, I said, "Why not?" I was glad that he let me do something for him. Tonight's birthday celebration was one he would remember.

What with the extra prodding and correcting from Richard lately, I wasn't sure where we stood. If I cared too much, I made myself vulnerable. Indifference wouldn't work either. Lately, the balance was off, or so I told myself as he backed his Mazda out of the garage and we headed for San Francisco. We were quiet traveling through Orinda and Oakland, but I didn't say, "A penny for your thoughts."

The only other time I saw the show, twenty-five years earlier, I took my mom for a Mother's Day celebration. Back then, I was teaching at Ohlone College, and one of the students I worked with played a role in the show. Was he thinking about past birthdays with Jean and Joan?

"Why so quiet?" I asked as we approached the toll plaza.

No answer.

We were on the bridge before he said, "There's no easy way to ask this." He didn't take his eyes off the road.

"Ask what?" Did he want something different for his birthday? Or want me to stop writing? Was this about the ring?

"I need to borrow money for payroll." He said it in a flat, factual voice. We both stared at the taillights on the car ahead.

My biggest fear had come true. He needed money and he had nowhere else to turn. He ran his business week-to-week for thirty-one years. When I didn't say anything he added, "I hate to ask but the checks haven't come yet."

"Um. How . . . much?" Though I wanted to be reasonable, I refused to be a fool. Visions of women loved only for their money passed through my head as I waited for his answer.

If I said no, I'd feel selfish. If I said yes, I'd be setting up unreasonable expectations.

"How much?" I asked again when he didn't respond.

"Sometimes I can't pay full wages until a job is done. The men are used to it. I need five thousand, but if you can't do that, three would be enough. I need something to give them."

"You can have the whole amount." I could have kicked myself. The words bypassed my brain and tumbled out of my mouth. If there were any resentment in my tone, he'd hear it. *Help.*

Even though I wanted him in my life, I would not take on his debt. It was too big, and we weren't young kids just starting out. Surely my dead parents were looking over my shoulder and warning me not to be sucked in. Since I didn't want his debt to be a deal-breaker, it was time to be cautious and diplomatic.

Even though I kept my financial matters private, he was savvy enough to know that I could afford to cover payroll. We were partners, or we were working towards it, and maybe this was something partners did for one another. He needed the money. Otherwise, he wouldn't have asked.

Obviously he sensed my hesitation because he said, "It would just be a loan. I'll pay you back in a couple of weeks."

Although he meant it, every warning I read in every woman's magazine with an article on the subject suggested that loaning money complicated relationships. The line between generous and gullible was smudged. But I didn't want his workers to have to wait for their wages, so maybe this would be a practical test of how good his word was. On the other hand, I could imagine the headline: "Intelligent Woman Squanders Savings!" I didn't want it to describe me.

Life was full of deals. But this? A loan to a friend who wanted to put his second wife's ring on my finger? What was I committing to, what were the future implications, and why was I still concerned about putting a damper on his birthday?

Leaning back, I lifted my head and saw the spires on the Bay Bridge from a brand-new angle. It was the first time I had ever crossed it at night in a convertible. It was so exciting to look straight up and see the sky and the stars beyond the top of the bridge that I mellowed out.

If we were partners, he made a reasonable request, I decided. If the checks hadn't come, he couldn't pay. I remembered all the people who warned me, "Never loan more than you can afford to lose." I could afford to lose five thousand. Once.

"I can do it."

"Thank you, dear," he said, and proceeded to tell me how to get a cashier's check so that I would have a copy and a record of the loan. He was borrowing money and telling me how to make it available to him. Fear stirred inside me as I listened.

Soon we were crossing Market Street and zipping around with a full view of all the buildings towering overhead. Miraculously, he found a parking space for his little Mazda in crowded North Beach. We walked into the theater with a few minutes to spare.

I was proud of the way Richard took my arm as we walked in. We had good seats and, once the show started, I could feel him putting his financial troubles aside. The costumes and the singing voices were fabulous. The hats were crazier than ever. Songs had been rewritten to include the latest political issues. We relaxed and laughed and thoroughly enjoyed the show and our front-of-the-house seats.

Afterwards, we stopped at a small Italian restaurant in North Beach. Richard's youngest daughter had taken the whole family there on another trip to the same show, he told me. His first wife, a singer, had been with them. As he got lost in the family stories, I heard both history and perspective. His kids grew up in an emotionally honest home, where they could come to their dad without embarrassment. Whatever their problem, he had once been in their shoes. But he was also someone with firm standards and rules. They always knew where they stood with him, because their actions had consequences.

When the kids needed money he'd say, "You want money? Sure. Go out back and pick some off of the money tree." He expected them to take the initiative and ask for work. Because he started mowing lawns when he was ten, his kids could certainly babysit or wash cars and windows. Rather than give them money, he gave them the pride that came from earning it for themselves.

* * *

The next morning, I went to my bank and got a cashier's check to cover Richard's payroll.

"You having some solar panels installed?" the bank clerk asked when I told her that I needed the check for an electrical company.

Richard's favorite excuse, "I couldn't say," wouldn't work this time. I said, "Not today," and she gave me the cashier's check.

Afterwards, I deposited it in the local branch of his bank. Partners helped each other out. Time to contribute. If I refused to lend, it would either develop into a thorn of resentment or plant an icy silence between us. He didn't want that. Neither did I. After a friend recently explained that if Richard wanted to get married, that put me in the driver's seat, I was curious to see if this would change us. Even if I was throwing away my hard-earned money, I made the right decision. Besides, Richard had promised to repay it, and if he couldn't, I wanted to know.

But still, he told me that he didn't want my money; yet here he was, asking for it. My mind churned. How could I be with him without assuming his debts? The answers would have been obvious if this were fiction. Instead, this was real life, and I didn't want to spoil it with a mistake I could not reverse. I needed to talk to someone who could explain how both relationships and loans worked in real life. Any intelligent person would tell me that no two cases were the same and I had to trust my own judgment. Life had become less predictable.

How simultaneously exciting and scary was that?

CHAPTER 16

ONE MORNING IN early October, when I sat on the floor brushing Mikko's curly shih tzu hair, my cell rang. Caller ID told me it was Richard. The corners of my lips turned up as I said, "Hello."

"I'm sitting in my car outside Burger King."

I could picture him in his Mazda with the top down, smoking a cigarette. "Okay."

"There's a man in a run-down car with bald tires and rust holes in the frame, and something told me to go across the street and talk to him."

I nodded, even though he couldn't see it. Not that it mattered. He went right on talking, the way he did whenever he was excited about something.

"He said he lost his job and only had two dollars left."

"And?" The economy was down, after all.

"We had a good chat. Afterwards I pulled out my wallet, took out a twenty, and said, 'I reckon you need this more than I do.'"

Something inside me softened. He gave whenever he saw a need, even if his business was facing financial trouble. Impractical?

Probably. Also, wise. He was always willing to help those less fortunate. He told me once that it was a huge part of his purpose on the planet. No wonder he never had any savings.

Without thinking I said, "If you want to, you can give him another twenty from me. I'll pay you back when you get home." The words skipped from my heart into my mouth, and bypassed rational thought and all the protections I'd been brought up with.

Financially unwise? Of course, since I just gave Richard five thousand a few days earlier. What message was I sending him? That I was a soft touch? That I could match his giving? That I needed to be his equal?

Though I hesitated to spend money, Richard thrived on it. Opposites attract. I wasn't sorry that I blurted out my offer or trusted my instincts. It was only a twenty, and that amount was huge to the man in the rusty car. But one of us had to be fiscally responsible.

What if money issues rather than kitchen issues would be our undoing? I shoved the thought out of my head. Richard wasn't going to let anything break us up. Marriage was for life, and he didn't know how to be happy without a wife.

When we first got together, he said, "Do you know how much baggage most women your age bring to a relationship?"

Not really. Blended families were not part of my experiences. My baggage was different. Doubts and fears sprouted like mushrooms in the undergrowth. Saying my fears—even my lifelong fears—were baggage would have been absurd. I didn't talk about that part of my history very much.

Now that I had loaned him the money, I had to take a second look at the two of us and our finances to be sure that I was not adding to either my guilt or my baggage. I had to be aware of the potential for loss and repercussions.

Richard was aware of my financial advisor. I trusted her judgment, so I called her and said, "Something has changed. There's a man in my life."

"That's wonderful. Who is he?"

"His name is Richard. He's an electrical contractor, and on Sundays he's a pastor." There was pride in my voice as I described him. I explained the great divide between our financial situations.

"Sounds like you need a prenup," she said.

Prenups are for Hollywood stars, I wanted to say, though I knew it wasn't true. Two of the women in my free writing group had them. They were for people who remarried or people who married late in life. If I didn't protect my nest egg, I might not be able to pay my monthly condo fees, utilities, clothing, gas, food, and medical care. Worse, if I lost it, I didn't have the energy to earn it back. Prenups were also for couples who planned to keep their assets separate. Plenty of sixty-somethings did that.

One night over dinner Richard told me, "Someday, I'll inherit some money. My father will divide everything equally, and I'll get a quarter of whatever's left after the medical bills and caregivers are paid."

"That's good," I said. Medical expenses can mount up in the last years of a person's life.

I didn't tell him that my financial advisor suggested I find an attorney. Instead, I googled the woman she recommended. According to the office website, she was the founding member of a firm that specialized in estate planning. I left a message with her receptionist, who I pictured sitting behind a marble counter in an office with muted colors and indirect lighting.

When the attorney called back, I gave her the thirty-second version of my situation. "You're sixty-two? Why haven't you been married before?"

I wondered what that had to do with anything. I said, "I was busy teaching drama, running rehearsals, caring for my mother, and running Writer Advice." I could have said that I never met the right man. That would have been the logical, accurate answer. Just never occurred to me. Instead, she triggered an old, sensitive wound.

Who finds a mate at 62? What was wrong with me? What did her question have to do with protecting my assets, and what was she trying to find out?

The attorney, an older woman with graying hair according to her website photo, told me, "Anything you earn after your marriage will become community property." That mattered. Someday, my investments might earn interest again, or Richard's business could thrive. Then he would owe me fifty percent of all his profits—if we were married. I couldn't imagine him allowing that, especially since he worked for thirty-one years to build his business for himself and his son.

"You'll both be required to fill out documents that fully disclose your assets and debts," she continued.

"That would be awkward."

Sensing my hesitation, the attorney added, "Maybe you shouldn't marry. Why don't you just live together? Many people in their sixties make that choice."

Though she couldn't see me, I shook my head fiercely as I thanked her for the advice and hung up. No way would I be taking it. Living together was not an option. Richard was a pastor. If we weren't getting married, he'd move on.

Besides, there had to be a way to keep us financially separate. How did other couples in their sixties resolve this issue?

Richard had recently told me about paperless marriages when we were driving on Northern California's back roads. "We'd be married in the eyes of God, but not in the eyes of the state," he said. "Is that enough for you?"

"Sure. As long as we say vows in front of a pastor, we'd be married." It was an easy solution. And I loved it because he did not want me to be legally liable for his debts.

I remembered the rebelliousness of couples in the Sixties and Seventies, who resisted state-sanctioned marriages even though they stayed together for years. Many were left-wing rebels defying the government. Not Richard. He served in the Navy during the very early years of the Vietnam conflict. In his own way, he had been a rebel since grade school, entertaining the class, taking risks, and testing the boundaries. He did it to get attention. There was no connection to any political protest.

"Is that enough for the church?" I asked.

He sighed before he said, "Not sure. I'll check with the senior pastor for this region." Richard had known him a long time, and we both trusted his judgement. A couple weeks later, we ran into him at a church supper.

After a bit of small talk, Richard introduced me and said, "Lynn and I want to get married. I don't want her saddled with my debts. You know how it's been."

He nodded as he sat on one of the benches next to us. He had a kind face and an engaging smile that was easier to see now that he was seated.

"We want to make it a paperless marriage. Would you have any problem marrying us if we did that?"

He shook his head, and smiled at me. "Of course not. The important thing is getting married. I'd be happy to marry the two of you. Now let's go get some food."

If we had a paperless marriage, we could share whatever we wanted, whenever we wanted. We would not be responsible for each other's debts or assets. Easy. Richard cared about being married in the eyes of God, and he was satisfied. His congregation and his kids would be, too. We could have an ordained minister marry us and be legal in our hearts.

Richard held my hand as we went to the buffet table. I filled my plate with potato salad, pasta salad, green salad, and chicken, while he filled his with every kind of meat available.

The problem should have been settled. However, the next morning my indecision returned. I couldn't believe it. "How can Richard and I merge our lives?" I asked Mikko without expecting an answer. Apples and oranges don't mix, and we were apples and oranges in our energy levels, our intellectual interests, and our movie and book choices, as well as our finances.

As I took a deep breath, I thought of the student who once told me that apples and oranges mixed fine in a fruit salad. Each had its own place, and they work toward a common goal—feeding people.

Once again, the whole relationship seemed plausible—until I remembered Richard's belief that the man had to be the head of the household because the Bible said so. Maybe that had been nagging at me, just under the surface, all along.

Richard explained that we would be partners and make all decisions together, and he would only use that authority if we had to make a choice and could not agree. If that were the case, he would make the final decision.

No way, I wanted to scream. His defense—*It's in the Bible*—wasn't enough for me.

I allowed him to be in control whenever the outcome didn't matter to me, and that was more often than I ever expected. He used to say that if we were buying a car and I wanted the red one and he wanted the blue one, we'd purchase the blue one because he was the head of the household. Why would that even matter when we had separate cars?

"Where do you want to eat?" he often asked over the phone, during his late afternoon calls.

I shot the question right back. I picked my battles, and the choice of food wasn't one of them anymore. We split our meals, and I usually allowed him to pick the food. I could supplement later and save on calories.

He reciprocated by asking my opinion and trying to please me. He never played the head-of-the-household card that he believed he carried.

"If Mama ain't happy, ain't nobody happy," he said more than once. He also told the church members that when he had the last word, it was *Yes, dear.*

While we were considering marriage, we also talked about finding a place closer to his business and his church, or buying land out in the country so he would have space to repair cars. It would have been a fresh start for both of us. We could have been equals in a new space.

Of course, if I sold my condo, I would never get back to Danville. Richard said that, in time, I would grow resentful. He knew I didn't want to change my life just to meet his needs, and that made me feel loved.

"The secret to a good marriage is no secrets," he said for the umpteenth time when we talked about moving. He encouraged me to say what was on my mind. That was refreshing.

"It's fine to keep the resources you're bringing into the marriage a secret as long as we both agreed to it," he reminded me. When he talked about not keeping secrets, he meant sexual secrets, and I didn't have any of those. He told me his history. He visited his doctor to be tested for sexually transmitted diseases, and he was fine. I was sure I'd never find such an honest man again. What was this thing I couldn't name that kept me in a state of uncertainty?

CHAPTER 17

A WEEK LATER, Richard woke up and sprang out of bed as if hit by a thunderbolt. "I can't live here anymore!"

What? No more sleepovers? I thought that was what he wanted.

"I had a dream. I have to move out." It was all perfectly clear to him.

"What? Why?" It was too early in the morning for this.

"How can I tell Brenda she can't live with a man when I'm living with you?"

Brenda was a church member living with the man she planned to marry. Applying the same standard to everyone meant that we could not share a bed, even though we weren't having intercourse.

"Oh—kay," I said, dragging out the word in a sleepy voice. I lied. It was far from okay.

"We're not breaking up. I just can't live here," he said. "We'll still date." Once, I thought this was what I wanted. Now it unnerved me. The only way to stop him would be to marry him.

Dreams have power. A few of mine have predicted the future. As a high school junior, I dreamed about a letter of rejection from a summer theatre program at Northwestern University. The letter came two days later. I was rejected. The same thing happened when I applied for the drama program at Carnegie Tech. More recently, I dreamed about emails telling me that I didn't get a speaking engagement or contract or residency, and within twenty-four hours an email showed up telling me what I already knew. I had no way to change the outcome once I had the dream, and I was grateful that I received a warning from the universe before the actual message. So, maybe Richard's dream was a prediction of some sort.

I watched from my side of the bed as he came out of the bathroom, dressed, and stuffed shirts, jeans, and underwear in his bag. He took his printer, his laptop, and his coffee to the car. "This feels like we're breaking up," he said as he gathered his blueprints off the dining room table. Complete flip-around from what he said less than an hour ago.

"If we were breaking up, you'd be storming around and I'd be crying." What a cliché, I thought, listening to my calm voice. I wouldn't be crying unless I believed he was gone for good, and I wouldn't start until he was out the door. In addition, he wouldn't be storming around. He was the most patient man I'd ever known.

Despite that fear, I didn't try to change his mind. We needed more answers. Would he accept living in Danville, or would he resent the commute? Would the condo stay in my name? Would I have to learn to deep fry his food? How much compromising would I have to do, and could I live with myself if I did it?

He left some of his clothes and all kinds of food—sausage and popcorn and tamales that I would never eat. Clearly, he planned to come back. From now on, though, he would sleep in his trailer at night.

As he gathered up things for the last trip to his Mazda he said, "We can still do sleepovers."

Weren't sleepovers and living together the same thing? Just as I was thinking he'd do his own laundry and return my house key and wait to be invited before he came over, he changed the rules again. Frankly, I was clueless.

If his dreams made him realize that we couldn't live together as husband and wife without the benefit of marriage that was okay with me. I would be getting my place back. I wouldn't have to go to bed when he did. He decided to move in. He decided to move out without asking for my input.

I didn't go to Bible study that night. I'd already told him that I was substituting at Temescal Writers, a group I attended for years before we met. It met at the same time as Bible study. I drove home at ten that night, watched the eleven o'clock news with Mikko, and slept deeply.

The next morning there was no coffee. There was no concern about whether or not to fix breakfast. Sitting on the sofa after making my own coffee, I had complete control of the TV remote.

Flipping from news to reruns to infomercials to Lifetime movies and back, I decided that channel surfing wasn't as much fun as I remembered. I missed both the adventure and the tension of having a partner to care about. I missed Richard.

His ring still sat on my dresser. Feeling lonely was no reason to put it on, I warned myself in a voice that would have made the women's magazines proud.

That night, I fed and walked Mikko before I ate some Lean Cuisine from the box. Sitting alone in front of the TV, just like the old days, I did not have to split my meal. I was concentrating on the news when my phone rang. Richard wanted to see how I was doing.

We chatted a bit, each of us alone in our own space.

"How was your day?"

"Fine. Yours?"

"Fine. What are you doing?"

"Working on a bid in my office. I haven't been home yet. You?"

"Talking to you." I didn't mention that I was enjoying the quiet. I respected him too much for that. Besides, it wasn't completely quiet.

The TV was on a news program instead of an action-adventure movie, and I had the company of the voices in my head. Tonight, they were only questioning a couple things.

Did he want me to stop him when he said he had to move out? Did he hope I'd change my mind about wearing the ring so it would make sense for us to live together?

As soon as we got off our cells, I did my dishes. He probably dumped his coffee and placed the dirty plate on the stack of dishes that already filled the sink right next to his grease-coated stove. I wasn't a cleanliness nut by any stretch of the imagination, and I sometimes rationalized that his eyesight was bad and he probably couldn't see the dirt and grease. Still, it was nice to have a clean kitchen.

The evening stretched out in front of me. I didn't go to a movie alone. I didn't look on Craigslist. Instead, I allowed my mind to wander wherever it wanted to go, did some email, read a book without interruption, and went to bed on the side that had been mine before Richard moved in. No one crowded me. I luxuriated in my space.

The next morning, I woke up alone. I was thoroughly rested after a second snore-free night. Only the sheets had touched me. I made my own coffee. I fed Mikko, and as I walked him, I considered calling Richard. At that exact moment, my phone rang. I grabbed it, saw his name on the caller ID, and my heart quickened. "Hello." I heard the smile in my voice.

"Would you like to go to dinner and a movie tonight?" he asked.

"Why not?" It was just dinner. He made the move, not me. Why didn't I put the ring on and admit we were engaged?

The same old reasons: fear around finances and my craving for the freedom to run my life my way. Maybe we'd talk about a compromise over dinner.

We met at a franchise café with a menu I liked. The one in Dublin had a Cobb salad, which Richard never ate, and they paired it with a honey muffin that was absolutely scrumptious. I was shocked when

I saw that this café had frayed carpet and taped upholstery. Richard noticed the poor maintenance right after he looked at the lights to see if they were using LEDs—an occupational hazard, because his company works on tenant improvements.

He asked me what I'd like for dinner. I told him about the Cobb salad. We compromised on a bowl of soup and pot roast. Compromise? I think not.

And here we go again.

I got so sick of being corrected. To avoid it, I usually said, "What would you like?" Only, that bothered him too. He wanted to give me choices. Sometimes it seemed like he did that so he could explain why my choices were wrong. That probably wasn't his intention. It just felt like it.

Clearly a man who didn't listen to me wasn't the right choice. Except that he did listen—whenever he remembered to. Impulsivity often took over rational thought. He could be charming, whenever his focus was on me instead of his business or church.

He was just being a man. My women friends told me that all men were this way. They started blowing off my specific complaints, as if to say that this behavior came with the territory. There was a lot that was good and right about him, and I had my own flaws.

At the café, the waitress served our food, he split it, and after we'd taken a few bites, I asked, "Where would we live if we got married?"

I could see the surprise in his eyes. He didn't know that I was just collecting information. His original plan was to move into a rental and share the cost. I explained that I didn't want to pay rent when I owned a condo in a neighborhood I liked. Why not stay there?

Instead of launching into the merits of a bigger kitchen this time, he asked me again, "Will you marry me?"

"Maybe. Probably. I appreciate your asking, but we need to figure a few things out first."

"You reckon?" His beaming smile warmed my heart. "We found a pastor who will give us a paperless marriage. I won't have you assuming my debts."

"I know." We'd solved that already. However, it wasn't our only issue. I asked, "Seriously, don't you think it's too soon?"

I should have asked if I could be an equal partner and pick my own food. The second issue had been resolved in his mind, and the first was a matter of interpretation. His version of equal was not the same as mine, as he had clearly explained more than once.

"Why should we wait? We're not kids. I love you. You say you love me. We're compatible. We're both Christians."

And even though he didn't say it, in the back of my head I heard, *you know what happened to my last girlfriend when she hesitated too long.*

I waited for him to ask me if I preferred being alone. He didn't, and to his credit, he probably didn't think about it. He always focused on the positive, while my fears made me more doubtful, introspective, and analytical.

Maybe he was right. Maybe it was time for me to put on the ring and see what it felt like to commit to someone. Maybe that would quiet the voice in my head that reminded me of my upbringing and warned me not to give my savings away. I was tired of being so unsure of myself. I was even more tired of feeling stuck.

CHAPTER 18

RICHARD CONTINUED ASKING me to marry him. Either I changed the subject or ignored the question. Though I cared for him very much, something wasn't quite right, and I still couldn't name it.

Then, one morning in November when he spent the night at his place, he called me up and his voice was bubbling with excitement. "Guess what," he said, and went right on without giving me a chance to respond. "I got into my car and reached for the pack of cigarettes I just opened. It wasn't there or in my pockets, so I checked the console and the glove compartment." He said it all in one breath. "I even went back inside to see if I left them on the counter. When I couldn't find 'em, I put out a fleece."

A strong proponent of trusting fleeces, he believed that they showed what God wanted you to do. In the Book of Judges in the Old Testament, a man puts a wool fleece on the threshing floor. He tells God, "If there is dew only on the fleece and all the ground is dry, then I will know that you will save Israel by my hand, as you said." The next morning, the ground was dry and the fleece was damp, so he had his answer.

Because I don't trust fleeces as much as Richard, I didn't say anything. No problem. He was too excited to hear me. "If I put the new pack of cigarettes in the garbage can, I told the Lord I'd give up smoking. So, I walked over to the garbage can, opened the lid, rummaged around, and sure enough, there they were."

"So, you're giving up smoking?"

"I promised God. I've made a doctor's appointment to get the patch, and until then I've found a way to cut back. I'll show you when I get home."

"Get home?"

"Can I come for a sleepover?"

Giggling I said, "Of course you can, little boy."

Three days after Richard said he had to move out, we started having sleepovers again. No surprise. As long as we didn't do it every night, this was okay again. Why? I never asked.

When we were together that night, he lit up a cigarette, took two puffs, and said, "Watch this." He took the remaining cigarette, put it out in the lid of one of his pens, and stuffed it back in his cigarette pack. "Two or three puffs are enough to satisfy me. I'm still not ready to quit cold turkey. I'll get my patches from Kaiser in ten days."

He continued to sit on my leaf-strewn back patio and smoke in a cushioned, iron chair that my parents had purchased when they were setting up housekeeping. True to his word, though, he always put the cigarette out after two or three puffs. Belief is a powerful thing. The jury was still out on whether I would ever use a fleece in my own life. If it gave him a reason to stop smoking, I was delighted.

The next Sunday, he told people in the church how they could taper off with two or three puffs just as he was doing. Most of the congregation were smokers at that time, and we ended Bible study early on Sundays so that people could grab a smoke in front of the church before the service started. "Smokers are a dying breed," he told church members, clients, and sometimes strangers more fervently than ever.

No one wanted to be chained to a habit, and smoking was an odious one—especially in California. I liked seeing the whole church support each other, and fewer and fewer people hung around outside between Bible study and preaching, as Richard called the service.

Once Richard got his patches, he gave up his two or three puffs and switched to Tic-Tacs. They were a great substitute for nicotine. Almost every day, I bought him a couple packages, and he bought far more. While he was driving, he would pop a whole handful into his mouth and ask me to pour more into his hand. Why not? I was honored to support his effort. One night when we met up for dinner he told me, "I reached for a cigarette today, but I pulled out the box of Tic-Tacs instead."

Fastening my seatbelt in his Mazda, I nodded.

"Without even thinking, I put a handful in my mouth and reached for my lighter."

"So you lit up a Tic-Tac?"

"I tried to. The flame almost burned my nose."

How could I keep from laughing? Addictive habits caused such absurdities.

I had smoked for three weeks in college before I quit. How I loved being part of a group and a subculture. I became automatic friends with others who lit up. I belonged simply because I had something in common with people who were so much more hip and cool than I was. Who knew that being accepted could come so easily and unexpectedly? Inhaling made me feel sophisticated. So did letting the smoke out slowly. So, this was why people smoked. Salem Menthols had a minty coolness, which soothed me. As I began craving more cigarettes, fears and doubts crept into my brain. My father's smoking was hard on both his health and his relationships. What if I liked smoking as much as I liked M&M's? Was a new addiction looming? No way. I stopped while I could. I didn't want to waste time on this new obsession. I was only three weeks into my habit when it was time to quit.

Richard started smoking in high school because smoking in the bathroom and behind the shops made him cool. The habit continued while he was in the Navy. Though he quit when he married Jean, he took it up again, smoked with Joan, and was set in his ways when we met.

This time, he quit at exactly the right time. Before long it would be too cold to sit on my leaf-strewn patio, puffing away and depositing the ashes in an old crystal ashtray that my dad had used. When Richard quit, he said it was because he wanted to live longer to spend more time with me. I loved his reasoning, and it was one more indication that he truly cared about me.

"Did you know I'm proud of you?" I asked when he'd been on the patch for a week. My statement was a rephrasing of his favorite line: "Do you know that I love you?" Being proud of him was a way of showing that I loved him without parroting or deferring to him. That was becoming my new bad habit. I had to fight it. I was too independent to defer to a potential husband unless I truly agreed with him.

Daily, I weighed our compatibility as well as our love. Although I enjoyed having my space, my heart fluttered every time I saw his name on the screen of my cell. Each time I picked up, there was a smile on my face and anticipation in my heart. If he asked me to a movie or a meal, I said yes. If he paid for the meal, I'd ask if I could pay for the movie. Asked instead of offering. That made him more comfortable and seemed fair. I continued to hope that we would be partners instead of him feeling a responsibility to be head of the household.

Being with Richard was a major switch in my lifestyle, and our adventures poured new energy into my life. Making room for him in my condo and attending his church didn't feel like concessions, as long as I also stayed involved in organizations like the American Association of University Women and Story Circle Network. I refused to give up the free writing group I'd been with since 2003, and insisted on reaching out to writers around the country through the online classes I taught.

Often, it was hard to take his advice when I preferred my own way of doing things, and even harder not to justify my actions. When he quit smoking, though, his advice was aimed towards others. I could sit back and enjoy his journey. He did it for God because of the fleece, of course. He also did it because he wanted to spend his remaining time with me. That was the kind of gift that made him loveable.

When we talked about our relationship, Richard often said, "God put us together."

Nodding, I would reply, "No argument from me."

One clear, sunny day long ago, as I was walking Mikko in the park under a cloud-free blue dome, I asked my God, "Isn't there some man—any man—who'd like to share his life with me?"

He brought me Warren, a memorable man who left this world too soon. The next time I went on Craigslist, he brought me Richard. Both men had less education and more life experience than I did. Both had been married and craved companionship and more. For a while after I met Richard, I wondered if God truly knew what I needed. It didn't take me long to figure out the answer, even though I found it hard to believe.

Remembering my original request from several years earlier, I now asked, "Is this your will, God?" as Mikko and I climbed the wide stairs that led up from the condos and into the park. Although I didn't hear *yes*, I didn't hear *no* either. Instead, the picture of Richard and me standing together in Yosemite came into my head. How I loved our beaming smiles.

CHAPTER 19

IN NOVEMBER, RICHARD'S oldest daughter, Jena, invited us to come to New Mexico to spend our Thanksgiving at her new place. She and her husband had moved from Arizona to help care for a two-year-old she called Little Man. Apparently, she marched to her own drummer. Reminded me of her father. After hearing many stories, I was eager to meet her. Should make for an interesting holiday.

Most of the passengers on our Thanksgiving flight were relaxing with a drink or a movie or a nap. The tense ones probably hated returning to strained relationships and the home where adolescent awkwardness and fights haunted them on every trip. Thank goodness I was beyond that.

As we passed the security boundaries in El Paso, crowds of people waited to hug relatives. Before I met Richard, I teared up when watching families reunite for the holidays. This time, I was with my friend—make that my almost-fiancé—and we were on a mission as we wheeled our suitcases through the hum and bustle of the crowds.

"Let's get out of Dodge," Richard said, heading for the rental car counter. "Want to try driving a mid-sized car before you buy a new one?" he said, although I didn't plan to buy a car until my Camry wore out, and he would be the primary driver on this trip. He didn't know that I drove my mother's Park Avenue Ultra for six years after she quit driving. I already had the experience he sought for me.

Even though we were putting the car on my credit card and I would have to sign the paperwork, Richard stepped up to the desk. Not a problem, though once it would have triggered resentment. He knew far more about cars than I did, and it was fun to watch him handle this transaction.

After I signed the charge slip for the Avis clerk, we searched the parking lot, stowed the suitcases in the freshly-vacuumed trunk of our assigned car, and Richard dug his GPS out of his suitcase. He was eager to see Jena and her husband, Eddie. Both Richard and Eddie were veterans of the Vietnam War, though Richard participated towards the beginning and Eddie fought close to the end.

Jena, or Nana as her grandchildren called her, was a mother, painter, bingo caller at the Disabled Veterans Hall, sometimes a DJ, and sometimes a caregiver. I couldn't wait to meet this free-spirited woman that life had tamed, watch her father and her together, and meet Eddie.

Their new home was an hour west of the El Paso airport. We traveled through the stark, cactus-strewn plains of eastern New Mexico to get there. Solitary, scrubby plants and low ranch houses had vast amounts of desert sand between them. Interstate 10 took us so close to the Mexican border that we saw the Sangre de Cristo Mountains on the southern horizon. I stared at tumbleweeds that had blown into fences and an occasional lone tree as we got closer to Deming.

We pulled into the driveway of their rental. Richard ushered me in to introduce me to Jena. Little Man stood by the refrigerator playing with magnetized plastic letters. He loved pulling them off and putting them back on, adored their shapes and bright colors, and especially enjoyed calling out their names and hearing, "That's right."

He pulled off a lime green *K*, held it up, and announced, "*X*."

"No," Nana said with exaggerated patience. "That's *K*—not *X*." She turned to me with a potato in one hand and a peeler in the other, and said, "We've been fighting since I gave him the letters. *X* is not a *K*."

He pulled off a blue letter, held it up and said, "*I*."

"Yes," she said, and his grin lit up the kitchen. Little Man loved Nana's approval.

Eddie was struggling to get Jena's washer and dryer to work. After Richard poured himself a cup of coffee, he joined Eddie, while I offered to help Jena. She didn't need any help, though. I sat at the kitchen table, watching and listening to the Little Man and Nana Show.

Richard discovered that the washer and dryer weren't working because of an electrical problem, and he needed parts to fix it. I did not know then that the two men fixed something together on every visit. He came into the house to tell us that they were going to the hardware store.

"Can I go along?" I asked.

"Why?" Richard eyes widened.

"Because I need cough drops and want to see what the choices are." The sand and relentless wind, bending the sagebrush until it was uprooted and turned into tumbleweed, had stirred up my allergies.

"Come on," he said with a reluctance that made me wonder if I was interrupting some male bonding ritual.

The hardware store was vintage. It had dirt-stained linoleum floors and metal shelves that reached nearly as high as the fluorescent lights hanging by chains looped over beams. Richard made sure Eddie got everything he could possibly need at the hardware store, and Eddie made sure he got a receipt so he could take back anything he didn't use. When the clerk said "That will be $179," Eddie's shoulders sank.

When Richard saw that he asked, "Would you re-add that?"

The clerk did, and Eddie put the $179 on his charge card and carried the package out.

Next, we stopped at Pepper's, a combination grocery and drug store. An indifferent clerk showed us to the correct aisle, and after looking at the unfamiliar brands of cough drops, I purchased a bag and popped one into my mouth before we were out of the store. By the time we walked into Jena's kitchen, I could swallow with ease.

Her stuffing was now prepped for Thursday morning, and Wednesday night's dinner was ready to serve when we walked in. She thrived in her kitchen, and Eddie handled the after-dinner cleanup with ease. They seemed like an ideal team.

* * *

The next morning, when Richard and I were getting dressed, he whispered, "Can you be sure you get packed so we'll be ready to go?" That surprised me for two reasons—he always waited until the last minute to pack, and we almost never left on our weekend getaways before dark. I did not ask, though. Like him, I was eager to see what was down the road.

Fifteen minutes later, I walked into the kitchen and headed for the coffee pot. Jena was dressed for the holiday with a big red bow in her hair and dangly earrings. She scowled as she dumped a heaping spoonful of coffee into the coffee maker.

Guests bring tension, and as soon as Richard filled his cup and headed for the garage, where Eddie was already working, I asked if she was all right. All she would tell me was, "Sometimes he makes me so mad. Not Daddy," she added when she saw my worried look.

A more confident woman might have asked what happened, or asked to talk about it. Even if I became her stepmother, I wasn't going to advise my husband's adult children unless they asked for my opinion. She had not done that. Besides, she would let it spill as soon as she was ready.

Jena sometimes mirrored Richard's controlling behaviors. Something had happened without her input, probably the $179 charge on their joint credit card. I never had to deal with unexpected charges on a credit card, so I had no idea what I would say if she asked me what to do. I understood that even compatible, comfortable husbands and wives have issues from time to time. She was a strong, decisive woman, who confronted whatever challenges came into her life. Richard and I had not had these problems. If we ever did, I hoped we would talk them through and resolve the issues. I hoped stubbornness and pride would not get in the way.

Listening to Jena, something inside me shifted. I was on an adventure this Thanksgiving. I didn't even want to direct it. I was along for the ride.

I had felt the same way one night before the trip. We were at El Nido, a restaurant in Danville. Richard was eating his taco and burrito, and I was making my way through my enchilada and the Spanish rice on the combo plate we were sharing. I had no idea why I once resisted Mexican food, apart from the fact that it was sometimes too spicy. Thank goodness I was moving beyond concerns about the food I ate. I'd decided that it was nice not to have to make every decision, and I felt the same way on this trip with Richard.

Jena's phone rang. She looked at the screen and asked me to keep an eye on Little Man. We went outside and I rolled his red-white-and-blue plastic ball through the weeds. He grabbed at it and squealed with the most delightful grin on his face. He squealed again as he picked it up. His sounds were carried away by a gust of wind that blew across the desert.

I kept thinking about Jena's generosity in taking care of Little Man, the son of a woman with drug problems she met while she worked as a DJ. Then her problem with Eddie popped into my head. I'd never been caught between a father and a husband, and that might be the issue here.

I never found out who was on the phone, but he or she frustrated

Jena to the point of tears. Despite her red eyes she maintained her Thanksgiving cheeriness when she came out to get us. Little Man ran between the kitchen and the living room while she stuffed the turkey and translated his words, which were spoken in Toddler-ese. It wasn't until Little Man went down for a nap and Jena had finished stuffing the turkey that she said, "Eddie makes me crazy. He always has to be right."

Some girls marry their fathers.

"Do you wear earrings?" Jena asked, abruptly changing the subject before I could respond.

I touched my ears. "I've never had them pierced."

"I could do it for you today. All you need is a potato and a needle, and I have both."

I'd heard about infections that resulted from this kind of piercing. "I don't think so."

She went right on as if she hadn't heard me. "I love to give earrings for gifts. I make them myself. Get your ears done soon." So like her dad. When I grew up, nice girls didn't have their ears pierced. Now, it had become a standard American ritual.

She took me into the bedroom, where she modeled some of her beaded, feathery designs for me. Her strong artistic sense came from her dad. As I stared silently at Eddie's knife collection, which hung over the bed, she talked about buying and stringing beads. Though the knife collection would have scared me, it didn't bother her at all. Of course, she was used to it, and showing off her earrings restored her good mood.

I took Richard aside when he came back in the house with Eddie a few minutes later. "Do you know what's going on between the two of them?"

"Something. Eddie wouldn't talk about it."

If Richard couldn't get him to talk, no one could. Eddie disappeared into the bedroom. Richard poured a cup of coffee. Jena put Little Man down for his nap. I waited.

Little Man was awake by the time his grandparents joined us for dinner. A graying couple, they seemed both hardworking and tired. Little Man was in his high chair when Jena asked, "Dad, would you carve?"

Richard's face glowed. He picked up the knife and plunged a fork into the juicy turkey. A second later, he stopped, turned to me, and said, "Will you take a picture of this?"

"If I can." Though he had shown me how to use it many times, his cell phone and I did not get along. He set it to shoot, and as soon as I took it in my hands, the home screen came up.

I had my own cell and would have used it, but Richard called my flippy phone a boat anchor. Shortly after we met in July, he wanted me to become accustomed to his and offered to add me to his Sprint plan. Wanting to maintain responsibility for my own phone and my own plan, I turned him down. After all, he wanted an independent woman.

Because I was shooting into the afternoon light pouring through the kitchen window, I could only get his darkened profile. I didn't want him to be a blob against the New Mexico sky. Though he would accept my efforts however weak, I wanted to demonstrate that I was a good photographer. I snapped shots from every angle I could, and tried to get Jena, Eddie, and the kitchen into the background.

I wanted natural shots. They wanted to pose. Once I explained that natural shots would be more authentic, they let me do it my way. So, maybe I had my own control issues, just like everyone else in the room.

After we were all seated and Richard said grace, we helped ourselves from the steaming bowls of food. Jena was used to cooking for crowds of family and neighbors. While I was helping myself to more dressing, Richard leaned over and whispered, "It's time to go."

"Dinner isn't over," I whispered back.

"We want to find a motel before dark." He pushed his chair back and stood up. Now I understood why he asked me to be packed before dinner.

He was already out of the kitchen, and about to load up the car. I turned to Jena and said, "He thinks it's time to go."

She nodded. "He gets restless."

She could be just as forgiving as her father. Her face was serene, despite a kitchen full of dishes, a table full of Thanksgiving guests, and a father who was leaving before dessert. They had their visit, and she met the woman who might be his next wife. We got along well, and she was at peace. If she was content and he was content, then he was also right—it was time to go.

Besides, I was eager to get to our next stop: Roswell, New Mexico. I had been curious about the museum containing evidence of aliens landing in a farmer's field in 1947. Would I feel a tingle in the air, or see some sign in the surrounding mountains proving that aliens crashed into the desert?

If I was so curious, why hadn't I visited the place years earlier? There were several reasons, and they made me realize why Richard would be an excellent partner. Going to Roswell alone seemed like too much effort, but going with Richard was easy. Alone, I would have no backup or resources if anything went wrong. How could I explain this venture when my friends would laugh? If I took someone with me, it seemed more legitimate.

Once I met Richard, anything became possible. When he asked me to share expenses, he also asked what I wanted to do in New Mexico. I checked the map to see how far Roswell was from Deming and told him about my secret desire to see the town where space aliens might have landed.

"Let's do it!" he said with the same enthusiasm he had for any new adventure. So, on Thanksgiving afternoon, while others sat in recliners watching football or reruns of the parade, we pulled onto a nearly empty highway and headed for Roswell, the landing place of aliens.

CHAPTER 20

THE SUN CAST long shadows across the desert as we drove between Deming and Las Cruces. I caught fleeting glimpses of families eating turkey, mothers scraping gravy from the roasting pan, and multi-generational groups stuffed with turkey and dressing, staring at the TV.

Jena was right. Richard was restless. Me? I was more curious. I always loved looking through open curtains—especially on holidays when everyone was dressed up and families were creating memories. It was like peering into a storybook and collecting snapshots.

Since Richard was driving, I could pick up when my cell phone rang. "Hello?" I said, not recognizing the number.

"Lynn? How are you? It's Cate." Cate was a friend who lived in California but moved to Tennessee to take care of her ailing mother several years earlier. She led the group I met David in. Now she spoke with panic in her voice. "What am I going to do? I don't have a job and I owe two thousand in taxes."

Because she had faced repeated health issues, she couldn't work. Without the money, she would lose her mother's home. She helped me after I had shoulder surgery—this was long before I even knew Richard—and I wanted to pay her back, so I offered to help her move to Tennessee. Her packing took forever, and by the time she was ready to leave, it was too late for me to go with her. I had commitments, so I wound up shipping her things to her instead.

My life had changed and so had hers. "I don't know if I've told you this, but I've met a man. We're on a trip right now, and . . ."

"I really need the money by Monday. Do you think you could go to a bank tomorrow and send me a cashier's check?"

"Um . . ."

"I wouldn't ask, but I really need it. I'll pay you back." She meant it, even if she had no idea how.

When I clicked off the phone, I told Richard about this slice of my life. "Do you think it's okay to lend her two thousand?" It was the first time I asked his opinion on whether I should spend this much, and I cared what he thought, even though we were talking about my money.

"Will she pay you back?"

"I think so . . . if she can."

"Do you think she's taking advantage of you?"

Ironic question given the money he borrowed for payroll a few weeks earlier. Or was I being paranoid? I'd loaned it willingly. Both of them needed the money. Richard had promised to pay me back. Cate hadn't said she would, though it was implied.

"A long time ago, I told her to let me know if she ever needed anything. At that time, I hadn't had anything better to do with my money."

"If you can afford it right now and it feels right, then you should do it. She doesn't have anyone else to turn to."

He was right. Technically, I could afford it. I'd contributed to movies and dinners and trips with him since we met, and could take the cash out of my Writer Advice account, which was all my own money.

But wait! Everything I had was mine, not just the one account. Strange hesitations still lurked around my money. I called her back and told her that I'd overnight her check no later than Saturday. If I could find a Wells Fargo in Roswell.

* * *

The next morning, Richard dropped me off in front of the UFO Museum in Roswell and parked the car. The stucco building looked like the front of a converted movie theater, complete with a marquee and pictures of aliens that matched the short, leathery-skinned creature with big eyes featured in *E.T. the Extra Terrestrial.*

Once we were both inside, we stared through glass cases to read the official government letters. Each writer had seen an alien or corpse in 1947. None of them told their story until on their deathbed, but several confirmed that an alien life form landed in a farmer's field outside of Roswell. Supposedly government officials swooped in, hid the evidence, and stashed the corpses somewhere deep inside a federal facility.

Richard stared at the displays, peering in and reading carefully. He never skims. "The government had to cover this up," he said after giving the letters careful scrutiny.

He saw for himself what I'd been saying about this place. We were thinking alike. Chalked up one more reason why this might work out.

Roswell had as many souvenirs as official documents, and after we bought a magnet for the refrigerator and a new travel cup for me, we headed for Carlsbad Canyon. Richard had visited the cave once with his second wife. Because of her heart trouble, she couldn't hike to the bottom of the cavern, three miles from the surface. Hearing that, I considered the descent into the cavern as a personal challenge, even though I was no hiker.

"Are you sure you can do this?" he asked as he parked the car. He was just being cautious.

"Absolutely." I didn't have Joan's heart problems, and both adrenaline and willpower would carry me through.

Together we started down a slanted, cement walkway, and about halfway down, I noticed everyone else zipping past.

"It's fine to go around me," I told couples and families.

We descended through the jagged rocks, stopping to stare at formations that had been lit to look like a Christmas tree, a metropolitan skyline, and a snowy monster reaching out with tentacle fingers.

Once we started down, there was no turning back, which made me doubly grateful for the handrail. I looked for emergency exit signs hidden behind the geologic formations. If they were there, I couldn't find them. After a while, I didn't care. About halfway down, my knees became wobbly. My right hip started hurting. We stopped often, took the best pictures we could without flash equipment, and when we reached the bottom, I collapsed on a bench. I was tired and triumphant when the elevator doors opened. I hadn't walked three miles in years.

At the gift shop, we bought another magnet. Then we returned to our rental car, and drove until we came to signs advertising Christmas on the Pecos, a forty-five-minute boat trip that showed the lights and decorations on some of the loveliest homes in Carlsbad.

"Want to go?" Richard asked with the excitement of a fifth grader.

"I want to, but the wind is going to freeze my ears off, and I don't have a hoodie."

Richard did, and he was planning to wear it, but he also brought his heavy gray jacket, and I had sensitive ears. "I don't think I can go without it," I told him in a pleading and pouty voice, and he relented, giving me his sweatshirt.

Though it felt wrong to be dependent on his kind nature, I needed the warmth that jacket would provide. For the first time, I understood why women sometimes pleaded or flirted to get what they needed. Life is a bartering system, I told myself that evening as I pulled the drawstring on his hood before we set off down the river. I tied it so tight that my face barely poked through.

My ears still got cold, but his sweatshirt allowed me to imagine myself as a teenage girl at the high school rally, who felt a little better than everyone nearby because her boyfriend's letter sweater was wrapped around her. I'd never worn anybody's letter sweater in high school. Now I couldn't stop grinning, just as I had in the Yosemite photo.

"Thank you," I said as we pulled away from the dock. "I hope you're not too cold."

He gave me a grin that said *You owe me*. Aloud he only said, "I'm not."

"I didn't think you would be. After all, you're the man."

Flagrant ego feeding, or feminine flattery? Did it really matter? Bartering was fun—especially when I got what I wanted.

When boys became important back in the seventh grade, my social status plummeted. I didn't understand why having a boyfriend made you popular. Or maybe I simply resisted the change in dynamics. Though I occasionally craved attention from boys, I never felt a burning desire to pair up with one. Instead, I went into some kind of gender-neutral zone. I wasn't a tomboy, but I didn't experiment with makeup or roll up my skirts at the waist. My body was changing and my mind was stuck. Seventh grade was the year that I got straight As, not the year I discovered boys. For the first time, I didn't measure up. Socializing was not taught or measured in school back then, and everything about it remained a mystery.

If I had stopped maturing emotionally as a teenager, I was making up for lost time by wearing my sixty-seven-year-old boyfriend's green sweatshirt. It was tangible proof that someone other than my parents loved me. In my mind, that sweatshirt broadcast his love to the whole world. But how sad that I was comparing myself to a high school girl wearing an athlete's sweater to a football game.

As we traveled down the river, we saw reindeer, stars, and wreathes illuminated with hundreds of tiny, white LEDs. Richard told me that this low-cost, high-output light fixture was the wave of the future. I'd heard it before. As we traveled farther down the dark river, his face lit up like a fifth grader. Look at this! Look at that! We kept saying it to each other as the lights outlining the Christmas gifts, bells, and sleighs sparkled around us. About halfway through the trip, he leaned over and whispered, "I love you."

"I love you too." My smile showed that I meant it. I didn't promise to love every single thing about Richard on every single day.

We rounded another corner with beautifully-lit homes and yards. He sighed and said, "It must be nice to have money."

I didn't know if the owners of these homes had bigger incomes, smaller families, or less overhead. Perhaps these homeowners spent their money in different ways. Or they had more saved before they got married. Or they saved before they went into business.

At sixty-seven, Richard still had aspirations and unfulfilled dreams. That was so much better than being bored, frustrated, or retired. He wanted to know what it felt like to have a house on the river and decorate it so that people would pay money to pass by on a boat tour and see what he'd done. He wanted what he had never had. So did I.

Despite his sweatshirt, I wrapped my arms around my body, and he rested his arm on my shoulder. By the time our forty-five-minute trip was over, we were both shivering. The tour owners had coffee and hot chocolate on the dock to warm us up. We both had coffee, of course. Our beverage tastes were a perfect match.

CHAPTER 21

STILL COLD, WE sat on a bench by the Pecos River, sipping our coffee. Out of nowhere, Cate's call on Thanksgiving night popped into my head. Here Richard and I were having a wonderful vacation, and she had no money.

When I mentioned traveling in New Mexico with a man I met four months earlier, she must have been shocked. Of course, I didn't say that he'd already offered me an engagement ring—a used one, a hand-me-down. Why let her think I was settling or desperate?

How could I think that?

I wasn't settling, and I outgrew being desperate by the time I was forty. Was I embarrassed that I found his ad on Craigslist? I found Cate's activities group there, too. You meet all kinds of people on Craigslist. A movie called *The Craigslist Killer* told one story. One. There are all kinds of people—including decent ones—available on Craigslist, and if I felt any shame about meeting Richard there, it was because of old judgmental values that I was now shedding. Okay, trying to shed. Those old values were certainly not the truth.

Before we left Roswell the next morning, Richard asked if I'd thought any more about Cate's call.

"She needs the money," was all I said. Richard's relationship with money was different than mine. He lived week-to-week asking God for help with payroll. I picked up his GPS. "Let's find a Wells Fargo before we leave Carlsbad."

It was the Saturday after Thanksgiving, and we observed the locals in boots and jackets as we waited inside the bank. Everyone was withdrawing money. This was the big weekend for holiday shopping.

At the teller's window, I pulled out my card and asked for a cashier's check for two thousand. While she processed it, Richard asked where the nearest post office was.

"Will you be sending this to a relative?" she asked.

"No," was all I said, but I said it with a smile as Richard took my hand. Let her think that I was putting a deposit on a sexy December getaway. Let her tell her boyfriend about the old couple who were spending their grandchildren's inheritance.

Let her tell him that two people can be in love at any age.

At the post office, Richard stepped into a line that snaked into the lobby, while I grabbed a Priority Mail envelope and addressed it. As I put the check inside, I thought of him buying a meal for the man sitting against the stucco wall of a Burger King. The ease with which he invited strangers to tell their stories amazed me. One month he might use his truck and trailer to help a church member move. Another month, the church's benevolence fund might pay a Pacific Gas and Electric bill or cover the cost of a car repair. First, though, Richard made sure that the church had enough money to pay its own bills. More than once he preached that you have to make sure to take care of yourself before you can help others. I had done that, and I liked using my personal benevolence fund to help a friend.

In the back of my mind, I often wondered how much money I would need to take care of myself. There was no way to calculate how long I might live or what the economy might do.

Before I was ten, in the late Fifties, my mother was shocked to discover that I had seventy-five dollars stashed on my shelves. I saved my allowance. I was never going to be poor. Even though the depression had been over for years, my parents' recollections of that time left me determined to remain solvent. I continued to save in high school, babysat on weekends in college, and always saved ten to forty percent of every paycheck. Financial solvency equaled independence. Until I met Richard, I thought independence was the only route to happiness. Finally, I was seeing the wisdom in my father's advice: find someone you love to spend your life with.

Giving to Cate made me grateful. It also earned Richard's approval, but that was separate. I didn't need his approval any more than Jena did. However, his approval did make me feel good. How I hoped he would love me enough to let me maintain my independence.

We left the Priority Mail envelope with the clerk and I took the green slip that said return receipt requested.

Cate got the check in time to keep the tax people from taking her mother's property. Before the next year ended, she faced more serious health issues that left her completely unable to work. She would have paid me back if she had the money, and someday she may still do it. I see her posts on Facebook, and once, at Richard's suggestion, I asked how she was doing and when she might be able to repay the loan. I never got a response. Maybe she assumed that it was a gift. It was more likely that cash was as scarce in her life as it used to be in Richard's.

Richard promised to take care of me if my money ever ran out. Though I didn't think it would, it was nice to have a backup plan, just in case. He'd always managed to support a huge family and run a business. With him at my side, I didn't have to live in a world of absolutes.

* * *

As we returned our rental car to the airport on Sunday morning, I remembered the Eleanor Roosevelt quote: "No one can make you feel inferior without your permission." I found it on the wall at a holiday party for members of Cate's activity group. It was easier to hang out in the kitchen and help with food preparation than to listen in on conversations. I didn't mix well with the others. Sadly, I allowed people to treat me like an outsider.

Richard changed that, too. His confidence gave him an advantage over me anytime I allowed it. The choice was up to me. He gave me his approval every time he said, "I love you." He talked more honestly about love and forgiveness than anyone I knew. I lapped up his words like I'd been in a desert for weeks.

How I wanted to be able to open up the way he did. What made him so confident? In a parallel, fantasy universe, I could have asked him to transfer some of his confidence. Of course, that was not possible. I had to find it on my own.

A warm little spot glowed inside me as we returned to the El Paso Airport, turned in the rental car, and boarded a Southwest flight for Oakland. We were heading into the Christmas season together. I'd always wanted a boyfriend for Christmas. I was sixteen going on sixty-three, and Richard enjoyed both my wide-eyed innocence and my maturity.

CHAPTER 22

BACK IN DANVILLE, with Thanksgiving behind us, I visited my favorite Starbucks on the first Monday afternoon in December. The shelves were loaded down with Christmas coffees and red-and-green commuter cups. Behind the counter, baristas promoted specials.

Across the street, in the high school where I taught drama in the Seventies, kids were preoccupied with formal dresses for the Diablo Cotillion, or ski jackets for New Years at Tahoe. Teachers droned on about math tests, history papers, five-paragraph essays, and science labs. I would never forget the boy who was late to class because he had to have money for a limo for the Winter Ball.

"I don't know if you've ever been to the bank on a Friday," he said, "but the lines are incredibly long."

"Yes, I know," I replied, folding my arms.

He was the kid and I was the grown up. He believed he had more life experience than I did. He was wrong. In some weird way, he was also right. I never rode to a Winter Ball in a limo or visited a bank during lunch because my date preparations were urgent. That year, I spent Christmas with my mother. Bubbly high school kids and crowds at the mall only reminded me that my life was empty. No wonder my defenses were up—along with my sadness. If only I had my own family, bringing home Christmas drawings, baking cookies, and asking questions about Santa. Though I would have been delighted to have my mom as a guest in my home, spending Christmas at her house just reminded me of the gaping holes in my life.

In my Seventies drama classes, we performed seasonal improvisations. Each actor played a small child before switching roles and becoming a department store Santa. Needy kids, angelic kids, defiant kids, and an occasional character with cancer or special needs, along with drunken Santas, arrogant Santas, and delusional Santas, kept us occupied and entertained.

Improv offered a chance to explore, safely. Actors tried on characters, including the sad and impoverished, and then stepped back into their own lives. My actors—they were always actors in drama rather than students—seemed to have a better grasp on the world than some of my English students, or maybe I knew them better. Improv was good preparation for life's unexpected complications and joys.

Twenty years after I walked away from my last high school position, some of the best and worst kids still stayed in my head. These were the ones I had relationships with. They got under my skin, and they mattered.

Staring at the school from Starbucks helped me consider who I had been. Would I lose all that if I became Richard's wife? To marry, or not to marry, that was the question. Was this God's will, or was I deluding myself?

"May I help you?" the barista asked. I'd reached the front of the line without even realizing it.

"I'll have a Pike's Place, tall, with about an inch of hot water." Holding my thumb and forefinger an inch apart, I showed her. She was new, and I was one of thousands of customers.

As I sat at a tiny table by the window, I remembered my friends' warning: *Be careful.* Even though the women in my book groups and writing group were glad that I'd found a man, no one was convinced that Richard was the right one for me.

In all this time, I hadn't introduced him to anyone other than the women in my *Sun Magazine* group. He asked to join us one night for dinner and conversation, I checked, and they consented. When we walked in, I was worried about how Richard and the atheist in our group would get along. She never mentioned her beliefs and didn't use the *F*-word the whole night. I was proud of her effort. Though we talked about marriages and relationships, and the women spoke frankly, he wasn't asked for his advice or wisdom.

Later he said, "They certainly didn't hold back. It's too bad I can't be there for all of them, but I found you first."

"Guess so," was all I said, though I couldn't stop smiling. After that night, he had more respect for my interests. Maybe he came because he wanted to see a slice of my world, since I'd seen so much of his.

I took a sip of my coffee and opened my journal to write a letter. It was the best way to process my thoughts.

> *Dear God,*
>
> *Is marrying Richard your will for me? Is our relationship preparation for something else? Is it a way to remind me I'm okay alone? Why Richard?*

I listened. I heard nothing.

Why not Richard? He was good and kind and honest and generous, and he could fix anything electrical or mechanical. He liked to cook. That sent a shudder through me, because he kept treating me like a novice in the kitchen. I kept right on going.

> *Okay, our tastes in food are different. I like*

salads, and fresh fruit that doesn't have cups of sugar sprinkled over it, and veggies. I hadn't had a piece of red meat for years until our first date.

But there'll never be a problem with my snacking in front of him. And if I ask him to, he'll take those snacks away in a heartbeat and help me stop overeating.

But do I want anyone else in my kitchen? Am I willing to turn it into our kitchen? Do I want to clean up after he fries oysters? Are we both battling over control? Is that your plan, God? Are you trying to show us who's really in control?

His intentions are completely clear. He wants to get married. After all these years, I've found a man I click with. If I'm suspicious about anything, all I have to do is get his attention and talk to him diplomatically. He believes that honesty is the secret to any successful marriage.

Richard is convinced You saved me for him. Who am I to say? I know You exist, but I don't always understand how You operate. Nor do I know why it is so hard to hear you. God, are You giving me someone who will expect me to provide for him, or someone who will let me teach him new habits around money?

Is he even teachable?

That was rude and I crossed it out. Of course he was teachable. I watched him pour over directions and catalogues, and even the sales columns in Craigslist. He educated himself every time he made a big purchase.

Is he supposed to teach me how to cook with canola oil, fry in bacon grease, and snack on chips and popcorn, or am I supposed to . . . I don't know . . .

assume the role of housewife? You don't want that, do You? I mean, if You really do, I'll give it a try, but if You are the God I believe in, You couldn't possibly impose restrictions that will build up resentment without giving me a way to get past my feelings, could You?

Maybe You want me to adopt his lifestyle. Live simply. See the world in black & white. Let the man take charge and serve him.

Seriously? Is that really the role of women? Not that Richard is expecting me to do that, I hope. But are You?

I was overreacting and examining worst-case scenarios. But wasn't that what journaling was for?

My best drama students understood that when a character wanted something, he also wanted the opposite. I wanted to be a wife, but I didn't want to set a date for the wedding. I wanted to be married. However, I didn't want to lose the independence of being single. I wanted advice that sounded right. I was thinking too hard, and I was scared to follow my heart. If I let Richard go, I would always wonder what might have been.

God, as You know, I don't deal well with the unknown. Richard is the only pastor I've ever known personally. Do You want us to open each other's eyes and stay together, or expand each other's world and move on? I'm questioning what I once prayed for. How human of me.

In July, I told Richard, "I love you when I'm with you." I loved his energy, enthusiasm and humor. I resisted the bad jokes, the paper towels used as napkins, and the fact that he felt more comfortable in that grungy trailer than he did in my condo.

> *The picture of us in Yosemite showed me what love looks like. I only had to compare that picture to the one he posted on Craigslist to see how much we'd both changed. He stood up tall and proud instead of slumping against his Mazda with his arms folded. My face beamed as I stood with his arm around me. We were engaged in life.*
>
> *Did I love him or did I love the idea of being a couple and the possibility of wearing a ring on my finger? And if that was all I wanted, was I tampering with his heart? And what kind of human being would that make me?*
>
> *Every time I sat in his trailer the voices that said, "You cannot live like this," got louder. But a still, soft voice, which could be You, encouraged me to take a risk, travel the country with Richard, and keep my wits about me. Try marriage, they said, knowing that more would be revealed.*

I reached for another sip of coffee and saw kids with backpacks surging across the street. My cell phone read *3:17*. The boys would scoop up the rest of the chocolate chip cookies, or maybe a girl would buy one and split it with two other girls. They helped each other with algebra and French until they returned to the school for practice or rehearsal or their rides showed up to take them home. To them, I was an old lady taking up a chair that one of them could use.

As I closed my journal, I decided that together we could forge a new life without letting go of our memories or individual identities. As I stuck my journal in my purse and stood up, I smiled at the high school students pouring through the door.

CHAPTER 23

ONE DAY, NOT long after I wrote to God from the Starbucks next to San Ramon High, I went to my dresser and picked up Richard's engagement ring. Holding it between my thumb and forefinger, I stared at the diamonds in their rose gold setting. Moving the ring back and forth in the sunlight, the colors of the rainbow sparkled against the wall. They moved fluidly.

I slid the ring—at least I wasn't calling it Joan's ring—onto my finger. This time, it reminded me that I was not alone, which made me smile. It was a promise, an attachment, and a secret key that would open the world of women who had been chosen.

Eying my finger as I responded to emails, I felt a surge of power. I had been chosen. The ring sparkled, and I couldn't wait to see Richard's face when he saw it there. No way that would happen in a phone call. I had to wait until he came home.

As the day progressed, I found myself curling my fingers when I washed my hands. I set the ring on the window ledge to do the dishes, then snatched it back before it could slide down the drain, tucked it deep into the pocket of my jeans, and put it back on when the dishes were done.

"You're driving yourself crazy," I said to the empty kitchen as I slid the ring back on my moist hands. "Don't you care about the man more than the ring?"

Maybe I cared about both.

That night, sitting across from Richard at the Mexican restaurant where we were eating, I made sure that my left hand stayed in plain view. We were dividing our dinner when he noticed my finger. His smile lit up his whole face. "Does this mean what I hope it means?"

I nodded. "I'll marry you, but would you mind if I added a ring guard?"

"What's a ring guard?"

"An adjustable piece of metal that will keep me from losing it."

"I guess you can do what you want. I gave it to you. Why don't you have it resized to fit your hand?"

"What if my fingers swell? Don't you think it's better to leave it as it is?"

He said that he'd given it to me, but I still didn't want to damage his property. Besides, I was afraid to make the ring mine. He'd expect it back if the marriage didn't last.

He shook his head. "I don't know about these things."

Part of me wanted to reply with, "One ring doesn't fit all, just like one size doesn't fit all." I knew better. The sparkly diamonds against the rose gold were pretty. He'd given me a family ring . . . sort of. Maybe he read my mind, or maybe he read my heart, because he said, "I'll get you one of your own someday."

"I know you want to do that." Pause. Silence. "So, tell me about your day."

* * *

The next afternoon, I walked into Smith's Jewelers with Joan's ring on my finger. It kept slipping, and I was there to see about a ring guard instead of getting it resized. "Is this band gold?"

The clerk looked carefully as I held up my left hand. "Can you take it off?" He put on a classic jeweler's monocle and said, "This could be rose gold. It could do with a good cleaning."

I didn't tell him that it had been soaked in Polident a couple months ago and then sat on my dresser collecting dust. Instead, I asked, "Can you put a ring guard on it?"

"Sure. And we'll polish up the gold for you at the same time."

So, my instincts had been right. Polident was a poor substitute for jewelry cleaner. "How much will it cost?"

"It depends on the kind of ring guard you get," he said, pulling out some samples. I stared at them. I had no idea what would be right. "This would be good. It's gold and only costs twenty-five dollars."

"And the cleaning?"

He stared for a minute. My jeans weren't pressed and I wasn't wearing a designer t-shirt, an expensive watch, or classy earrings. "No charge."

He had turned toward the backroom when I stopped him. "May I ask you one more thing?" After lifting the lid, I removed my grandmother's engagement ring from the box hidden inside my purse. For a while, my mother wore it on her right hand. Then she got arthritis and swollen knuckles, so she put it away. I inherited it and wore it only once.

Standing there, I recognized a pattern in my thought. The same issue had come up with Joan's ring. Not really mine. My rational mind knew that it was. It just felt wrong, emotionally. Why? Neither my mother nor my grandmother would know if anything bad happened. Besides, you lose your attachment to property on the other side. "I've never had this ring appraised. Can you tell me what it's worth?"

He put the monocle back on, stared, squinted, and moved the ring back and forward. "We'd need to keep this a couple of days to appraise it."

"It's worth a lot more than the other one?"

"Oh, yes." He looked like he wanted to know where I'd gotten it, but was too polite to ask. Or maybe he was trying to be business-like.

"It belonged to my grandmother." I'd never met the woman or her husband. Now I had her ring.

"You want to take good care of this," he said, and that was enough of an appraisal for the moment. I tucked the ring back in its box and put the box in a zippered compartment in my purse. Before bringing it in I had shown it to Richard, who said, "You can't wear that anywhere. Someone would cut your whole finger off to get it. It's too big."

"Maybe people would think its cubic zirconium?"

"Maybe . . ."

When I got home from the jeweler's, I returned it to my dresser drawer and kept it there. I didn't want my grandmother's ring overshadowing my fiancé's.

That Sunday, during Bible study, Richard announced that we were engaged. A large woman at the end of the table said, "Let's see the ring."

Smiling, I held up my hand. A young mother sitting next to me took my hand in hers for a closer inspection and said, "Pretty."

Nobody asked, "Is that a hand-me-down?" Nobody recognized Joan's ring, even though many knew her. This was a time for celebration.

When I walked into the meeting of my *Sun Magazine* group the next week, I set my contribution for dinner on the counter as a woman asked, "What's new?"

I shrugged.

"Are you engaged yet?" another one asked.

I held up my finger.

"You've got a ring and everything," the first one said.

She wanted her own engagement ring, but first she needed to find the right man. I kept a tiny chuckle inside. Throwing herself at one man after another, as she did, wouldn't help. How I wished she knew that. Maybe some of the high school warnings about good girls and nice girls had been right. She was the flirt who put herself out there.

At that moment, I liked the ring almost as much as I liked my fiancé.

CHAPTER 24

WITHOUT REALIZING IT, I had increased the number of chores in my daily domestic routine. Almost every day, I washed clothes and filled the dishwasher. I cooked more often, using the stove instead of the microwave, still refusing to let Richard teach me to deep fry. No way I'd put up with hot grease splashing me or leaving its residue on the walls. Besides, I didn't want Richard consuming it regularly—not even canola oil.

We often ate out, which eliminated some hassles and hurt feelings. He continued to use lots of salt on his fried foods and everything else. I told him, "You are a medical miracle." One night as he finished his portion of the rib eyes we shared, I added, "You should be written up in the *New England Journal of Medicine*."

"Why? I'm not sick."

"My point exactly."

He looked puzzled.

"You're diabetic. You eat too much salt and sugar. You practically live on pistachios and potato chips and candy. You're still running your business, and you show no signs of slowing down. Given the diabetes and the way you lead your life, you are a medical miracle."

"Okay," he said with a smile. Though it was a compliment, the salt and grease could be silent killers. Maybe he was too close to his own good fortune to see it.

* * *

One Wednesday morning, as we ate breakfast in a favorite restaurant and talked about our plans for the day, my ring sparkled in the sunlight pouring through the window by our booth. I liked it more and more all the time. It gave me confidence. These were the perks of connection.

I went about my day, writing, running errands, and doing laundry before I left at four for Bible study in the northwest corner of the county. I got there early and was sitting in the Starbucks closest to the church when I looked down at my left hand and gasped. My stomach dropped. My whole body started to shake.

The ring was gone. It must have fallen off despite the ring guard.

Maybe it was on the street. Or someone picked it up. Or drove over it at the gas station. My hands kept shaking as I called the last place I was sure I had seen it—the restaurant. Maybe it dropped on the seat.

After four rings, a young-sounding hostess picked up.

I explained what I lost and where I'd been sitting. "Can someone look between the booth and the window?" I asked. "Maybe it slipped off while I was having breakfast. Can you check and see if it's lodged in the space between the cushion and the wall?" Without waiting for an answer, I continued, "We were two booths away from the door by the window, and I was facing the cash register and the door."

"We'll look after we close." Her answer was short and curt. It wasn't her ring.

"But . . ."

"We'll give you a call if we find anything," she said.

"Call me either way," I insisted. She'd hung up. They weren't going to find anything. I would have gone myself; however, I was across the county, and they were about to close. Besides, they could look more thoroughly.

What would it cost to replace the ring? And how would I feel about wearing a new engagement ring that I paid for myself?

This relationship was too costly. I had to pay for the ring and end the relationship before he asked for another loan or I paid for another dinner or deepened my emotional investment.

I went out to the car, where Mikko was waiting for me. We went on a walk to burn up some of the adrenaline racing through me. Before we got back to the car, I punched in Richard's number. "I'm afraid I have some bad news," I said as soon as he picked up. "The ring is missing. I mean gone. I'm so sorry. I'll get you a new one, of course. Do you remember how much it cost?"

The words came tumbling out so fast that he didn't have time to ask a question, much less tell me that everything would be all right or, heaven forbid, yell at me about my irresponsibility.

"Let's wait and see if it turns up," he said once I took a breath. He did not say it was okay or that I was forgiven. I hoped he understood that it was an accident. And probably he did. With audible disappointment he added, "Keep looking."

Or was he trying to be supportive? It bothered me that I could not tell. Usually, I was the one to hide my truths, and he was forthright—make that transparent. What if he considered it an omen and was too disappointed in me to say anything?

I was heading back to my car when the restaurant called. "We looked but didn't find any ring."

Stunned, I begged, "Please, look, again."

"I'm sorry. It's not here," the hostess said. She ended the call.

"What if someone took it?" I asked Mikko.

After we got home that night, I looked on the dresser. I looked on the nightstand. I looked by the sink. I looked on the rug around the toilet. I got down and ran my hand across the carpet. I looked by my computer and around my desk, and I flipped the sofa cushions and checked the counters in the kitchen and even looked inside the refrigerator. I took a flashlight and ran the beam up and down the walls behind the furniture. I was being ridiculous.

The ring was gone. I missed it. My connection to Richard was growing deeper, and I didn't realize it until my ring finger was bare again.

The next morning, I got up reluctantly. I trudged into the kitchen to feed Mikko, who was becoming more *our* dog than mine. Bending down, I reached for his water bowl.

Next to it, I saw something new on the linoleum. Something shiny.

My heart thumped against my ribs, and my hands shook as fiercely as they had the day before. Could it be the ring? Or were my eyes playing tricks? Without my glasses, who knew? *Probably a piece of scrunched foil,* I told myself. After all, I hadn't seen it last night when I fed him after we got home from Bible study.

I bent over and picked up the shiny lump. Turned out, it was round and flat and had a hole in the center. The rim was solid. This was not a piece of foil. Between my thumb and forefinger was the ring I had once rejected. I could have kissed it. Instead, I slid it onto my finger and reached for the phone to call my fiancé.

"I found it." My heart was still pounding. "I found my ring." I didn't say *the* ring or *her* ring or *your* ring. I called it *my* ring.

"I knew it would turn up."

Maybe he did, in some intuitive way. Maybe that's why he was so casual about it. Who was I to say? He didn't sound at all surprised as he asked, "Where was it?"

"Right next to Mikko's water bowl." It had fallen off in a safe place where I couldn't miss it. I'd been looking for signs from the universe, and I chose to see this as the message I'd been looking for. I needed to lose something in order to realize what I had. Richard and I were meant to be together.

No more resisting. I would never find someone like Richard again. My heart accepted that as true. How many electrical contractor/pastor/two-time widowers were out there looking for a third wife? Of those, how many would be willing to take a chance on a rookie who hadn't experienced the joys and problems of marriage? I wanted to overcome my inexperience. I wanted to move forward and see where marriage took me.

Richard accepted me, and now that I had my ring back, the feeling was mutual. We were a couple of good-hearted, imperfect, youngish seniors, partnering up. I was ready to be his wife, despite the voices that had taken up residence in my head and wouldn't stop warning me not to marry him. If I was going to move forward, it was now or never, and never was not an option.

CHAPTER 25

SOME PEOPLE MAY have a knack for shopping, decorating, and entertaining, or thriving during the holidays. Not me. I hated the crowded stores, long lines, and newly-trained cashiers. I always seemed to be pushing myself to beat the calendar.

Growing up, I felt like the whole shopping and decorating extravaganza avoided the real reason for the season. By my mid-thirties, the wall between Christmas and me could no longer be scaled. For me, December was the time to give to charity. After my mother's death, I spent the season huddled with my dog and the television. Richard promised to change all that. Though he had his work cut out for him, I secretly hoped that he would succeed.

It all started at the December meeting of my American Association of University Women (AAUW) film group, which Richard had joined two months earlier. By then, he was eager to know everyone involved in my life. He brought fresh opinions and a unique point-of-view. At his first meeting, he volunteered to calculate the scores of the movies we rated. By making himself useful, Richard fit right in. Besides, he was genuinely interested in everyone, and impressed by their knowledge.

During our December meeting, one of the leaders reminded us that the AAUW needed docents for all five houses for the Holiday Home Tour.

"In addition to docents," the leader said, "we need men to stand by a miniature train. We just want someone who can—"

Richard's hand shot up before the woman could finish her sentence.

Leaning over, I whispered, "Are you sure?"

"Happy to do it," he whispered back.

"Richard, that's terrific!" she replied with a beaming face and large smile.

Cars and trains were right up his ally. I loved his boyish enthusiasm, too. He would monitor the trains soaring down the tracks, troubleshoot electrical problems, and at the same time become friends with the people in my life. All in a single, two-hour shift. A week later, he donned a conductor's cap and babysat a miniature train with at least ten cars circling through a snowy village on miniature tracks.

When he returned, I smiled. "How'd it go?"

"Everyone was nice and friendly. I don't understand why the AAUW needed someone in the room. The trains ran like they're supposed to, and these people aren't thieves."

The AAUW placed conductors in the room to avoid liability issues and protect a treasured family heirloom from accidents. It was easier to ask the retired husbands to be train conductors than to find more docents.

"Did you have a good time?"

"Sure. It was fine for a one-time deal," he replied.

Richard could put a positive spin on any experience. And at the same time, he imposed a boundary. Clever man. No one trained him to do that. He was just hardwired that way. Unlike the other men who volunteered, he wasn't retired. Richard was still busy with his customers and employees. Though he was generous with his time to the AAUW group, the concept of retirement remained foreign to Richard.

When we talked that night over dinner, he said, "Would you like to go the AAUW Christmas party?"

He must have heard people talking about it while he guarded the train set. The last time I went to an AAUW party, the living room was filled with chatting couples. It didn't matter that there were other unattached women attending. It didn't matter that this was an association of university women. The experience convinced me that I was an outsider. I left almost as soon as I got there. This year would be different.

"Why not? If you're sure you really want to go."

"Don't you?" Richard tilted his head to one side and studied me.

How did he fit in so well? Whether it was a waiter serving us dinner or a man driving a shuttle to the airport, Richard engaged total strangers in conversations. It was beautiful to watch him learn their stories. I still held out hope that some of his skill would rub off on me.

With Richard at my side, of course I'd go to the party. Now, I would fit in. Instead of sitting alone in a darkened living room staring at *It's a Wonderful Life,* I would spend Christmas Eve at a party with my date—another imagined moment left over from my teens and twenties that would finally become real.

Never say never.

The corners of my lips turned up as I answered, "Sure. Why not?"

Maybe Richard saw something in me that I myself could not. In his mind, he could cure my old insecurities, despite the deep roots. All he had to say were those three little words.

"I love you."

With a total of forty-four years of marriage behind him, Richard knew more about lasting relationships than I ever would. I only read books.

The following Saturday, I worked as an AAUW docent, giving rides up and down the steep driveway of an elaborate home perched atop a hill bordering Mt. Diablo State Park. The energetic or physically fit walked or hiked. It was I who drove the elderly, the disabled, or the simply tired to the decorated front door of this elegant, Christmas-y mansion. As I turned the car around in the big driveway, I promised them a ride down if they waited for me.

After my four-hour shift I enjoyed a tour of the house. With high ceilings, creamy carpets, plush furniture, and tasteful holiday decorations, it was beautiful. I, however, would hate living with such pristine surroundings.

Resting on the front porch, I pulled the surgery booties off my shoes. We all wore them, except for those who left their shoes outside. For the last time, I drove down the steep driveway, accompanied by two elderly women, both in flat shoes and one with a cane.

Richard spent that Saturday in his office working on blueprints for the job he was bidding. Anticipating appetizers and desserts at the party, we skipped dinner. Richard dressed in his Johnny Cash outfit. The one he wore on our first date. With a red silk shirt, a black-and-silver sweater that I wore when my mother was alive, black pants, and Naot flats, I thought I looked pretty good. Once he programmed his GPS, Richard drove his freshly-washed Mazda to a posh court at the south end of Danville. The streets were lined with cars. When he finally spotted an opening, I was grateful we had taken his small sports car.

Someone had placed a money jar on a card table on the porch. The funds raised helped girls and women. I paid for Richard and me and made our nametags. My heart fluttered as we walked into the two-story home together, hand in hand.

Greeted by a curving staircase that dominated the front hall with a railing wrapped in wide, red-and-gold ribbon, our jaws dropped.

"Wow," Richard stated.

With elegant decorations, window treatments, a grand piano,

and a lit tree in every room, the home was the epitome of elegance. It was packed with men and women in party clothes. Clustered in groups with drinks in their hands, the guests chatted as we inched our way into the kitchen. The hostess smiled as soon as she saw us.

"You can put your coats in here," she said, showing us a back room.

"Wow," Richard said again. "You've got some nice lighting in here."

I laughed. By now, I could count on him to notice something as mundane as the lighting. Didn't matter whether we were in a home, a restaurant, or a museum.

Setting my old coat next to one trimmed with black fur, I laughed. Although AAUW members were politically correct and it was probably fake, the fur still looked real. I could afford a coat with a fur collar if I wanted one. Instead I made excuses. What would it take for me to feel comfortable about spending that kind of money on myself?

The answer came to me way too quickly—I needed to believe that I deserved nice things in my life.

Interesting how that glitch was also in the way of the marriage Richard asked for. As a child, I read stories about families loving each other. Together, they overcame poverty. In many ways, my middle-class world didn't seem legitimate.

Several men crowding around a counter filled with wine bottles nodded to us when we entered the kitchen. Women passed by carrying hors d'oeuvre trays. Everyone had something to do or someone to talk to. As I stood there, my old discomforts crept in. Feeling out of place, I was glancing at a television in the door of the hostess' refrigerator (you can't make this stuff up) when a woman called out, "How am I going to manage?"

As Richard rushed into the pantry, I followed. He just *loved* rescuing people. A long-time AAUW member and former elementary teacher stood with her hands on her hips. Pointing at a four-layer cake on top of a flimsy, pink cake box, she sighed.

"I don't know how to get this out and onto the plate without dropping it."

"Let's do it together," Richard suggested. He loved his kitchen skills as much as he loved helping. "Where's the cake plate?"

Pat, who was used to being in charge, pointed to it. Richard, who controlled everything in his world, brought it over, set it next to the box, and carefully slipped the cardboard tabs out of their slots. Together the two lifted the teetering cake, which sat on top of a heavy cardboard circle. Setting it back down again, they frowned. Somehow, they had to slide that cake off the cardboard and onto the pedestal without dropping it or sticking their fingers into it.

Richard turned to me and said, "Bring me the plate." As I did, he turned to Pat and added, "Now lift."

She did as he said.

"Lynn, slide the plate under, please."

I slid it beneath the frosted masterpiece. The heavy cardboard circle was still attached.

Richard and Pat both shook their heads.

"This won't work," Richard said. "We need a spatula."

I grabbed one. Pat balanced the cake plate. Richard deftly slid the spatula under a portion of the cardboard and wiggled it. The cake shook. What if the layers separated from the frosting or broke into crumbs?

"Grab another spatula. Grab as many as you can find." Richard's eyes stayed glued to the cake.

Two spatulas went to Richard, two to Pat, and I kept the last two.

"Put it there," Richard instructed Pat. Using his chin, he indicated a section of the cake. She followed his directions perfectly.

"And the third one goes . . ."

I was already on it, fearing that we were going to create cake soup.

Wiggling our spatulas—one . . . two—the cake separated from the cardboard. Richard and I lifted it with our four spatulas, and the cardboard dropped away. Pat slid the cake plate underneath without dropping a crumb.

How did we pull it off? Perhaps it was an act of will, or faith, or maybe Richard and Pat had enough confidence that there was just no way we could fail.

"Wow," Pat said, standing back to admire the achievement. "How could I have done this without you?" Staring at the cake with a broad grin that matched Richard's, she clapped.

Laughing inside, I imagined Richard as one of her students. When she was younger and still teaching, could Richard have been the boy in the front row who acted like he was the only kid in the room? "Teacher? Teacher?" I could just hear him now.

Richard had no clue that Pat had once been a grade school teacher with traditional standards. She might have been his nemesis. He might have been hers. That night, though, they were just two people handling one task. Now I wondered. Whatever happened to my most disruptive students? And Pat's? How many were now pastors? How many were in jail this Christmas?

When I first told Richard that I taught English and drama in high school and college, he replied, with mock seriousness, "I felt responsible for keeping my teachers and classes entertained. If I got sent to the principal, it was because the teacher moved her boundary."

His words rang oh-so-true. I'd been a teacher who moved boundaries when my students pushed me too hard, erasing the boundaries one question at a time. Why did some students insist on running the show regardless of anything I said or did? And what did it matter now? Maybe they had the same needs for approval and control as the man I was engaged to. How ironic.

A long time ago, Pat might have labeled Richard a class clown or a troublemaker. Probably during the first week of school. She would never have met the real boy behind the invisible label. Tonight, though, this retired schoolteacher and former class clown were a team. And Richard took the lead because he always assumed that was his job. He needed to be noticed. Too bad he didn't know that a real teacher was now deferring to him. Then again, she didn't know that a class clown was running the show.

What would my former students think if they knew I was seriously considering marrying a class clown? Irony meets entertainment? She's getting what she deserves?

Richard and I were living proof that opposites attract. I found an adventurous, fun-loving man I never knew I wanted, and I was proud to be engaged to him. Even though he'd given me his second wife's ring.

CHAPTER 26

AS WE GEARED up for the holidays, the store windows in Danville were filled with ornaments, bows, and giant candy canes. Richard brought home a small tree. We set it on the Duncan Phyfe drum table that my parents were given when they married. Decorating it with LED Christmas lights and ornaments my high school students had given me over the years, we made it uniquely ours. Six decades of my life had come together.

Since Richard didn't like artificial trees, my mother's smaller one ended up in my office. Its tiny white lights sparkled off the walls and ceiling, turning the plain white surfaces into a kaleidoscope of art. Gathering together my holiday trinkets, I placed my decorative angels throughout the condo. The hand-carved wooden ones were made in Quebec. The garishly painted ones were gifts from my students. The few that had arrived in the mail included a request for a donation. You can never have enough angels that silently bless a home.

On my mind lately? The need to shop for my great nephews and niece. The oldest, at seven, and the youngest, at two, lived almost a thousand miles closer to the North Pole than I did. Inventing stories about snowstorms blocking the reindeer or Santa being stuck in traffic would never fly with those little ones. Now December 18th, it was time to shop.

"What's the rush?" Richard asked.

Did we live on separate planets or something? What didn't he understand?

"The post office won't guarantee delivery if the packages are mailed after December 19th," I argued. "That's tomorrow."

"Okay," he replied, calm as usual. "We can pick up all the presents we need for both families at Target."

Simple solution. Buy four presents. Wrap four presents. Mail four presents.

When it came time to leave, I grabbed my purse while Richard poured coffee. When he offered to drive, I handed him the keys.

"What do you think about iTunes gift cards for Nathan and Emily and Haleigh?" he asked as we sat behind a stream of red taillights.

"Great. What about the younger ones?"

"Some kind of toy," he replied. "You've already figured out what you're getting, right?"

"A Nintendo game for Asher, a sports jersey for Carter, maybe a doll for Savannah, and something toddlery for Cooper."

We started with the jersey. Carter lived in a family of Giants fans. However, the Giants were a San Francisco team and the Target in San Ramon only had gear for the Oakland A's. Richard never sweated the small stuff. Therefore, for the younger kids he thought any shirt from a professional team would work. Although I disagreed, the clock was ticking.

"What size do you need?" he asked as I pawed through the rack.

"Five, I think."

"You don't know?"

Since when was he so precise? "I talked to his dad, but he's a man, and you know how they are."

Richard's jaw dropped.

"What's wrong?" I'd flipped one of his statements: *You're only a woman.* Something he usually said to get a reaction. Tonight, he heard that statement in a completely new way. And so did I. How excellent it felt to declare gender superiority even though the crowds in Target were making me nervous.

The truth was that men and women both had their strengths and their weaknesses. Richard would always have more upper body strength than me. He had endurance and an ability to fix anything electrical. I was the critical thinker who saw the gray areas, while he saw the world only in black and white.

Usually, I was more aware of nuances, subtlety, sarcasm, irony, and multiple layers of thought than he was. It only bothered me when he was missing something critical. I was lucky that he didn't mind hearing the truth, though he often ignored what I said. Maybe I did the same to him, too.

Richard's eyes widened behind his bifocals. "No one should classify an entire gender by saying *he's a man* or *she's a woman*."

No one. Not me and not him. Now that I placed a new spin on his statement, he got it. Previously, he admitted that I had more education, and I acknowledged that he had more common sense and street smarts.

When Richard explained that the man was the head of the household, I folded my arms and replied, "Not always."

Before I could cite even one example, he cut me off. "It's in the Bible."

That was the discussion stopper. It was in the Old Testament, and a large portion of the Old Testament was cultural. We would have to revisit that issue another time. Tonight, we had to shop, shop, shop.

I bought Carter an Oakland A's shirt in a size five. It was pragmatic. If Richard was wrong and Carter's parents couldn't explain that the Oakland team was across the bay from San Francisco, they could replace it with the correct jersey. We visited the toy aisles, where I found the recommended Nintendo game for Asher.

Together we found Transformer action figures for Jordan, Tyson, and Blade, three of Richard's grandsons, who were around Carter's age. I found a beautiful baby doll for Blade's sister, Ava, and a softer Raggedy Ann that would fit into a big mailer envelope for Savannah. We added them to the cart and picked up something with moveable parts, cute sounds, and bright colors for Cooper. At the checkout counter, we picked up the iTunes cards for the teenagers. And with that, our shopping for the grandkids was complete.

Shopping for Richard was a struggle. I had no idea what he wanted or needed. When I asked, he told me that he didn't know.

"I'd love to fly in a hot air balloon. Someday, maybe I'll learn how to fly a plane." He smiled as he talked.

Was he nine years old? Though I respected his big dreams, he wasn't getting any flying lessons for Christmas from me. A few months ago, I bought him some clothes.

"Think about what you really want," I said, and immediately added, "within reason."

"So, a trip to Italy is out?"

"Maybe someday."

A few moments later Richard said, "What about a boxed set of the Indiana Jones movies?"

"What about it?"

"For Christmas."

Grea-a-a-t. Action adventure. Just the right romantic touch. If I said it aloud, he would have told me, *you're having an attitude.* He hated my sarcasm. Instead I asked, "Don't you already have a couple of the movies?"

He went right on as if I hadn't said a word. "If you get a used one from Amazon, there might be something wrong with the disks."

"So then, a new box set from Amazon would be fine?"

"Might be expensive."

Okay. Maybe he was trying to make my Christmas shopping simple. Next year I could get him something more personal. This way I'd know he was getting something he wanted.

When I went online, Amazon advertised unopened box sets with a two-day delivery. Shopping online was easier, and that was an unexpected gift he didn't know he had given me. Or maybe he did. Maybe the fact that he kept it simple and picked something online made it somewhat romantic because I had more energy for other things.

The last time I watched an Indiana Jones movie, I was at a cast party following closing night of a show at the Dramateurs in the mid-Eighties. All I remembered was something about the hero saving a stranded girl. Maybe Richard imagined he was my rescuer. Did I even need to be rescued? If I asked, I'd probably sound whiney, or at least overly analytical. This was not the time to push those buttons. It was time to trust.

I lived sixty-two years without a rescuer and must admit that just his presence was reshaping me into a gentler, more loving woman. Richard loved both feisty women and compliant ones—make that *accepting* ones. Our relationship shifted both of our perspectives. One day at a time, I was figuring out how to give him what he wanted without compromising who I was.

CHAPTER 27

ON CHRISTMAS EVE day, I hung out in front of the TV. Richard went to work while I filled my day with reruns, coffee, journaling, laundry, and contentment. Richard's middle daughter, Beth, was a superb cook. In charge of the Christmas Eve dinner, she would be doing what she loved. Richard and I were excited to spend the time with her teenagers, her siblings and their kids, and a couple of honorary Browns. The more the merrier.

When I offered to bring something, Beth said, "Just bring yourself. You're our guest."

Their mother was gone and I was their dad's girlfriend. They were comfortable reminiscing about their past with me in the room. The improvised meals and activities that made them feel loved when their mom was alive filled their stories. I listened as they recalled English muffins and biscuit pizzas, family excursions, and the year their dad wired someone else's hot tub on Christmas Eve. They gave me a whole new picture of who Richard used to be and how he made his family work, even when times were lean.

I was on the computer when I heard Richard's key in the lock just before dinner.

"Come see what I've got." His youthful spirit made me smile. Carrying a stack of blue pocket t-shirts with the company name over the pocket, he proudly handed me one. His workers wore them on the job. "Try it on. I want to see how you look."

Holding it up, I turned it around. Then I saw the company logo and *Shorts Removal Team* emblazoned in huge, yellow letters on the back. Beneath it was a phone number.

"You wear this slogan?"

"People love these shirts. Girls are always asking me where they can get one."

I wanted to say I'm a woman, not a girl, and who are these girls and why do they like this sexist slogan? Then again, who could crush all that eagerness?

"I want you to wear it to dinner at Bethie's."

In my family of origin, we dressed up for Christmas Eve. After slipping the shirt over my head, I glanced in the mirror, combed my hair, and smiled.

What a way to announce our connection. His daughters knew their dad. Therefore, that slogan would be no surprise to them. More than likely they'd understand that my wardrobe choice wasn't really mine. Or maybe they'd think that making their dad happy was more important than what I wore. In either case, they'd be right. His sons probably wouldn't even notice what was on my back. Christmas with the Browns would be a new adventure for me, whether it was a one-shot deal or it became my new normal.

Richard noticed that I was staring into the mirror and said, "I bought paper and bows. Can you help me wrap the presents?"

The presents for my sister's family had been mailed the day after we shopped at Target. Richard's presents sat in the trunk of his Mazda until two hours before Christmas Eve dinner. No wonder he needed a wife.

Grabbing my Scotch tape, I pushed the stack of mail and books to the edge of the dining room table. I hoped that we had enough workspace. Together, we unrolled his wrapping paper. Metallic black flecks scattered everywhere.

"I can vacuum when we're done," I said, wrapping Transformers in assembly-line fashion, just like the elf crew at the North Pole. Holding the paper together, Richard slapped on the tape. I folded the ends, and Richard taped again.

Wrapping presents hurt my back. However, our assembly line made the work speed by. Wrapping for seven of his grandkids was actually fun. I couldn't wait to watch the paper fly around after the dinner.

Once we were finished, I massaged my back. Richard didn't notice.

Instead he said, "I left something in the cabinet above the upper oven. Could you get it for me?"

Did his question mark keep it from being an order? When I sighed, the grimace on his face told me that I was having an attitude. *Fine.* He was pushing my buttons, and I was pushing back. Even if I didn't say a word, my body language screamed *Stop treating me like your servant.*

Nevertheless, I reached into the cabinet above the stove. My hand touched paper towels, a hotplate I made in kindergarten, and bowls my mother inherited from her mother.

"What kind of package am I looking for?"

"It's flat and wrapped in tissue paper."

"What is it?"

"Don't you see it? Can you bring it here?"

More orders, phrased as questions. *Whatever.* At least I would spend Christmas with a big family instead of sitting in front of the TV and walking Mikko. Everything in life was a tradeoff.

My fingertips touched a wrapped package stapled with striped curly ribbons on tissue paper.

When I handed it to Richard, he handed it right back. "Merry Christmas. Open it."

As I sat down, his face lit up. Tackling the Scotch tape that held the tissue paper firmly in place, I smiled.

"Don't worry about the paper," he said.

Freckle-faced, pre-pubescent boys ripping into Christmas presents in a Norman Rockwell painting filled my head. Inside the tissue paper, I discovered an elegant necklace of pearls separated by carved blocks of gold that were decorated with miniature diamonds. The long strand sparkled under the dining room lights.

"Put it on."

It was long enough that I only had to lift it over my head. Looking down, I touched the pearls. Then I looked him in the eye and whispered, "Thank you." His eyes said he wanted more. Leaning across the table, I kissed him.

"Is there anything else?" he asked.

At first, I thought he wanted more than a single kiss. But nestled within the paper were two earrings that matched the necklace. They were lovely, but I couldn't squeeze the earring through the tiny opening in my left ear. My ears were newly pierced, so the skin was tender. I tried again. And again. I didn't wear earrings every day, so the holes probably had tightened up.

"I'm going to need help."

It was exactly what he wanted to hear. Tucking my hair behind my ears, he said, "Turn toward the light."

Richard struggled with the earrings, too, but he got them in. After a few seconds, Richard stood back and smiled.

"These are handmade," he said, standing behind me as I looked at myself in the mirror.

"They're lovely."

Although incongruous with the t-shirt, they were perfect in Richard's eyes. He was the first man to give me pearls. A pearl necklace with matching earrings. I kissed him again.

There was a lot to like about this man who wanted me to share his life. If only we could resolve our pragmatic difficulties. Today was not the time for thinking about our problems. Instead, I went into the office where I'd stored the Indiana Jones movie set that I ordered online. He was pleased, not surprised. Why would he be? Next year, I'd find him something more personal. By then, I would know exactly what he wanted.

* * *

With Richard's arms full of presents, we walked together to the front door of Beth's house. I rang the doorbell. When Sarah saw my shirt, she frowned. Dressed in holiday clothing, she was probably eager to see what I'd be wearing. A look of understanding filled her eyes a minute later. Obviously, she respected my choice. After hugging us, she ushered us to the kitchen, where Beth was pulling appetizers from the oven. Six-year-old Tyson held up his glass for a refill. Everybody's chatter drowned out the Christmas music.

Following the Brown family tradition, the older grandkids took care of the younger ones. They hung out in the living room, playing games and scrambling for the best chairs. The adults gathered around the dining room table a few feet away. Parents filled plates with enchiladas and tacos and Spanish rice for their kids, who were out of sight but not out of earshot. If they became too rowdy, one or more parents stepped in. A warning was all it took. Richard had passed his boundaries onto his kids, and they were automatically passing them on to the next generation.

As long as I was with Richard, I belonged. When they dug out pictures of earlier Christmases, I stared at the love in Jean's eyes as she posed with her kids. She'd been an amazing woman, raising seven children, putting up with Richard's quirks, and instilling family solidarity in everyone. It was easy for them to talk about their mom's strength, spirit, and zany humor in front of me. I soaked up every story.

We were halfway through dinner when Richard's second son and fourth child, Petr, showed up with his boyfriend. Despite Petr's unique perspective on the world—from the way he spelled his name to his refusal to work for the establishment—he ended every phone call by saying, "Love you, Pops."

Watching and listening to three generations of Browns, I could see why Richard didn't hold a Christmas Eve service. Christmas was a family time. Like an elastic rubber band, the Brown family could stretch to the limit and still bounce back. I respected the resiliency. Hopefully, it would continue to extend to me.

After dinner, we played the gift-giving game where you either pick a new gift or steal—in an open and friendly way—one that was opened by someone else. The kids had assigned gifts. Even after they opened their presents, they hung around coaching their parents on which gifts they should steal and which ones they should hang on to.

When my number came up, I looked at what was available, shook my head, and picked a wrapped package from the table. Opening it, I smiled. An Oakland Athletics pillow. Perfect for any fan watching the game at home. The Browns, especially Beth, are huge A's fans. I figured it would be stolen, and I couldn't wait to see who took it first.

Sam's wife, Mel, was next. Her son, Tyson said, "Take it," pointing at the pillow.

She shrugged her shoulders, held her hand out, and said, "I don't really have a choice here."

"That's okay." I eyed the open presents again.

Three people held up their gifts and said, "Don't you want this?"

"Couldn't you use this?" I took pity on Sam's twin, David, holding up a lovely, rose-sequined tote bag from Victoria's Secret. He had no use for the cosmetics inside, and I couldn't see him carrying the bag anywhere.

Taking the gift from David, Beth said, "If the gifts are too feminine, guys, don't have your wives do the shopping."

Way to go, Beth. The best cure for chauvinism among good

people was awareness.

I thought back to Richard reciting one of Jean's favorite sayings: "Behind every successful man is a woman, standing there with her arms folded, rolling her eyes." He'd said it with a smile and rolled his own eyes. He recognized the power a woman held to persuade, urge, and nudge. Although she was a devout woman who heard the Old Testament dogma many times, Jean knew the truth. Richard believed that he had the final say as the head of the household. We both knew that he could only be in control if I allowed it. Maybe I'd fit in just fine as a Brown wife.

After the presents, Richard stood up. That was our signal. He was ready to go, just as he had been at Jena's during Thanksgiving dinner. We gathered our coats and asked Sarah what time breakfast started at her house the next day. Then we were out the door, leaving the siblings to hang around for hours. As we stepped into the December night, our frosty breath danced in the air. We looked forward to whatever the rest of the night would bring.

CHAPTER 28

"WE NEED TO set a wedding date," Richard said to me after Christmas. "How about January?"

We'd had this discussion before. I shook my head, and said nothing.

When I was about thirty-five, my mother's upstairs neighbor got married a couple months after his first wife died. "Some men have to be married," my mother explained when she told me about his new wife. Though I was unsophisticated, I'd seen enough TV and read enough books to understand that some men had strong needs. There were men and women who could not tolerate being alone.

"Someday, you may get married, and that man might take everything you have." Her statement was so uncharacteristic that I assumed I misheard. "If he does, it's okay. I don't want you to worry about it." How could this generous, loving statement come out of the mouth of my cautious mother? Why wasn't she warning me to guard against such a thing? Of course that moment stayed with me.

Although I guarded my money and possessions, I never had to fight to hold onto anything. Back then, I believed I was mature.

Now, though, I see how emotionally naïve and inexperienced I really was. She wanted me to find happiness, even if she wasn't here to see it—even if I lost whatever she had left me. Did my mother assume my chances of getting married were slim to none? I never brought a boyfriend home to meet her. Maybe she felt bad about the discussions we never had about boyfriends and wise choices and love and marriage and living happily ever after. No need or any reason to have such a discussion. Maybe it was her way of opening up our talk about me finding a life partner. I saw a new version of my mother that day. Unfortunately, it was now too late to ask her anything. Did she have any idea how much that statement opened me up to seeking a man once she was gone?

* * *

Richard's daughter, Jena, called us one evening in February. He didn't have the phone on speaker, but their conversation was obvious. She must have asked about us, because Richard told her about my hesitations. As I left the room, Richard shook his head and motioned for me to stay. He handed me the phone.

"I hear you're having a little trouble planning your wedding," Jena said. "Let me help. The first thing you need to do is pick out your colors."

It was wise advice, I'm sure. As she talked, all I could think was *no. No, no, no.*

"And a wedding dress," she said. "Now, I'll need pictures. So, send them to me, okay? I'll help you pick it out."

A wedding dress on a sixty-two-year-old woman would look ridiculous. She meant well. However, having my future stepdaughter plan my wedding was beyond absurd. Why call attention to the fact that I never married and didn't know how to plan a wedding? Besides, I didn't want a dress, a bouquet, or the expense.

Richard showed me a picture of him walking up the aisle after he married his second wife, Joan. He wore the gray suit Joan had picked out for him to wear to Jean's funeral six weeks earlier. Joan wore a knee-length, flower-print dress.

Why get elaborately dressed for his third wedding? Richard watched me roll my eyes. Overwhelmed by her eagerness, I thanked Jena for her offer. Giving the phone back to her dad, I walked out of the room, shaking my head. I didn't want to be a blushing bride. If I were going to blush, I'd save it for our wedding night.

Jena's eager plans did help me realize that I didn't want to get married. I wanted to *be* married.

As soon as he got off the phone, Richard came into my office. "What's wrong?"

"I don't want to pick out colors or flowers."

He understood. "Let's say our vows in front of a preacher and skip the rest. Why don't we go to Reno this weekend?"

Was it possible that he wanted to be on the other side of all those marriage details as badly as I did?

"Maybe."

He kept pushing. I didn't push back. There was no one else like Richard. I didn't want to lose him; unfortunately, he wasn't willing to wait. My parents were married in a little church in Reno on the seventeenth of November. This Friday would be the seventeenth of February, and Richard wanted to go to Reno. Perhaps it was a sign that everything was falling into place, and I should just do this.

He cared about me. I cared about him. We both wanted to move forward with our lives. We were making a commitment to spend our days together as partners—husband and wife. We wanted to make that promise in front of God. Anything else, like a dress or a cake or bridesmaids or flowers or picking out colors, was nothing but cultural hoo-ha. I didn't want to revert to a childhood fantasy I created before I knew anything about relationships or marriage.

* * *

On that special morning in February, I sat at my desk, answering emails as if it were any other normal day. Tackling my to-do list, my insides quivered. Surely I wasn't going through with this. After editing a client's writing, I moved on to evaluating contest entries. Focusing on writing silenced the negative gremlins screaming inside my head. The idea of driving to Reno and saying marriage vows only remained surreal as long as I was busy.

I turned to Mikko. "Am I really doing this?"

Mikko had suffered a doggie-stroke two weeks earlier and still walked a little unevenly. Even if he'd been healthy, he wasn't a marriage counselor. He was more of a silent sounding board. If he could have spoken, he'd have said, "Do it if you want to."

Most brides didn't work on their wedding day, unless you count hair and makeup. I wasn't going to visit a hair salon. I did pack my purple sweater and the long skirt that went with it—clothes I bought for my nephew's wedding—even though I didn't want to dress up. Richard didn't care about my appearance. He wasn't on my case about my size or the fact that I usually didn't bother with makeup. He never called me unfeminine or judged me. Best of all, he never held up either of his previous wives as a measuring stick.

That day, Richard picked me up at six in the afternoon. We loaded my suitcase and his ditty bag in the trunk of my Camry. He lifted Mikko into the back seat. When he had suggested we go to Reno on Friday, he said we should bring Mikko because he was still recovering from his stroke. Maybe he thought that having my dog with me would make me feel more secure about marrying him. In doing so, he gave me one more reason to trust him.

We crossed the Carquinez Bridge, heading toward Sacramento as the sun slid behind the coastal mountains. The Lifetime movie about the Craigslist killer popped into my head. Ridiculous as it was, I decided to let someone know where we were going. I punched in Stacy's number. She knew more about my life and history than anyone. It was no surprise when she didn't pick up. Her life was full of responsibilities, so I left her a message.

The pine trees loomed overhead, darkening the road. Richard's headlights lit the way. We trusted the car lights, just as we trusted each other. Sixty-two years of training to be cautious stayed with me. At the same time, I was thrilled to be eloping in the tradition of my parents. For a couple about to be married, we didn't have much to say.

"A penny for your thoughts?" I finally said to break the ice.

"I was just thinking about all the cars that have LED headlights."

Was this real? We were on our way to a wedding chapel, and his focus was on headlights! No TV couple I ever saw was this complacent on their way to their own wedding. However, the shows had dramatic conflicts and high stakes. We only had two different histories and each other.

I couldn't turn the clock back or undo my past resistance. All I could do was see what happened next. Otherwise, I would never experience marriage. While I was considering how little we had in common, my phone rang. It was Stacy.

"Are you sure you want to do this?"

"Yes." I said it flatly.

"I always imagined Richard standing on one side of you and me on the other." Stacy spoke with compassion. As she did, I remembered the phone call with Jena and the horrible stress of pleasing everyone that I so desperately wanted to avoid. If I was to marry, it had to be before anyone had a chance to tell me their expectations.

"I just wanted somebody to know where I was going and what was happening," I explained.

"You don't have to do anything you don't want to do."

Take a risk or sit alone in front of my TV, my mind screamed out. Imagining my life after saying for better or for worse, I grinned.

There was a choice. Stacy was right. I didn't have to do this. I chose to. There's no other way to discover what lies on the other side of a wedding ceremony. Besides, I liked and trusted Richard and was sure that our love would grow.

"I want to do this." However, if I never make it back, call the police, my mind silently added. Absurd. I wasn't in a movie or in a book. It was real life, and Richard had no intention of getting rid of me. He was sitting right next to me, hearing my half of the conversation, and more than likely imagining my thoughts. He drove and probably wondered whether I would back out at the last minute. He was about to get married for a third time. What was that like for him?

"Everything okay?" he asked as I stuffed my cell back into the pocket of my jeans.

"Sure."

"That's good," he said. We drove on silently in the darkness.

Less than an hour later, we saw the lights of Reno. Richard handed me the GPS. "See if you can find us a wedding chapel."

The closest one was Arch of Reno on North Virginia Street. I punched it into the GPS. We would be there in twelve minutes. I still had time to change my mind. However, I preferred to change my life.

We found the chapel. Richard drove around the block before parking my Camry on a side street that had only two streetlights. He helped me out of the car like the gentleman he was. As I climbed out, I glanced around. No one was standing in a doorway waiting to attack. These were not the thoughts of a normal bride. Then again, when had I ever fit inside a traditional stereotype?

"We'll be back, Mikko," I said before Richard locked the doors.

"And you'll be married," he added as he took my hand.

Walking down Virginia Street, I reminded myself why we were doing this. Richard had asked me, and I loved the novelty of feeling chosen by him. He wanted me in his life. He wanted to be married and so did I. It was an old wish, buried under years of believing that I wasn't good enough or pretty enough. Richard lifted my self-imposed shroud because I gave him the power to do so. He confirmed what I always hoped: It was never too late to find true happiness.

His energy and enthusiasm, the approval I received from his

children, and the friendship from his church renewed my fading sense of purpose. Being a pastor's wife intrigued me. Would it be challenging? Maybe. Wasn't everything in life a challenge?

CHAPTER 29

AS WE WALKED toward the Arch of Reno Wedding Chapel, we looked like any other older couple—him in a ball cap and me in jeans. Lights from the storefronts and streetlamps dotted the darkness. No one would suspect that we were about to be married, much less that I was a first-time bride.

Once inside, I couldn't take my eyes off the rows and rows of photos on the walls. All ages, sizes, and ethnicities smiled back. These couples wore everything from formal dress to Western garb as they stood with their arms wrapped around each other. Where were they now? Were they still married?

A receptionist in a soft blue dress welcomed us. She looked as generic as the wedding chapel.

"We're looking for a place to get married," Richard said. "Do you have an ordained minister here?"

"I'll get him."

While we waited, I looked at the wedding rings protected by a glass case with a scratched surface. I sighed. I already had my ring—formerly known as Joan's ring. Thank goodness I found it by

Mikko's water dish after it disappeared. Richard could not afford a new one. On our way to Reno, Richard told me that he had searched his cupboards one more time looking for his old wedding ring. He couldn't find it anywhere. That was a relief. I didn't want him to wear a recycled ring when I could buy him a new one. Even more, I didn't want him reusing the ring a previous wife had given to him. Frankly, I was surprised that he even looked for it. I thought he would want a new ring to match a new commitment.

Of course, I hadn't purchased one yet. Why buy one when getting married seemed like an unattainable fantasy?

The minister walked into the office from behind a curtain. He and the receptionist wore huge smiles. He grasped Richard's hard-working hand in his much larger one. A tall man, he seemed sincerely happy to have us there. When he looked me directly in my eyes, a joyous bride did not look back. He gave me a questioning look.

I took his hand and nodded slightly, letting him know that I wanted this despite my reticence.

"The first thing we'll do is get in the limousine and take you to City Hall for your paperwork," the minister said.

I looked away.

Richard leaned in and quietly asked, "Is it possible for us to do this without going to City Hall?" We'd agreed on a paperless marriage. When I heard Richard speaking so softly to the minister, the whole thing sounded shady, even though it wasn't. Plenty of people were married this way—especially older people.

After contacting the attorney about a prenup, Richard reassured me that a marriage ceremony performed by an ordained minister was all we needed to be married in the eyes of God. As a pastor, he should know. We were two sexagenarians, not a young couple with plans to raise children. He was a grandfather and I was a great aunt.

"Is this a recommitment ceremony?" the minister asked.

I looked at my husband-to-be, who grinned. "Something like that." It was a recommitment to marriage and love for him. That was clear. "We just want the ceremony. Are you an ordained minister?"

"I am, and I've been doing this for the last six years." He again looked into my eyes, as if he felt a tacit need to ask, *are you sure you want to get married?*

I was prepared to live with my decision, even though I was too old to be a starry-eyed bride. At the same time, the receptionist stepped up and said, "We have some lovely wedding gowns."

I almost laughed. The last thing I wanted to do was dress in a costume for this show. We didn't have an audience or a congregation or even a couple of witnesses to stand up for us.

"No thanks, but Richard needs a ring." We picked out one made of titanium that slid smoothly on his finger. After he took it off, I placed it on to my thumb for safekeeping, promising to buy a better one when we returned home.

After walking down a darkened hallway, we waited in the light from a low-wattage, bare bulb. Standing in that corridor we could have been backstage in the old Little Theatre at San Ramon High. While we waited, I looked carefully at what we were wearing. I wanted to remember. He was in his green, striped shirt and black jeans. I wore my blue jeans that we purchased in Texas and a red-and-black sweater old enough to have yarn pills on it.

We hadn't had time to change. It was already ten-thirty and we didn't have a place to stay yet. Not to mention, the wedding chapel closed at midnight. We weren't having pictures and that didn't matter anyway. I wanted a picture in my head. I closed my eyes and imprinted the two of us waiting by the chapel onto my brain cells.

I didn't say a penny for your thoughts. If I had, I believe he would have said something about the lighting. Much later, I learned he was thinking that I just might back out. He presented himself with so much confidence that I had no idea.

The receptionist in her blue dress came down the hall. Who was covering the front desk? She pushed a button, and a recording of the wedding march from *Lohengrin* played. I smiled up at Richard, as if to say, here we go. He smiled back. We were definitely partners now.

He took my arm, and when the receptionist signaled us, we walked down the aisle together, passing a dozen empty pews. He was playing the roles of both father and groom in this wedding. Somehow, it fit.

At my request we skipped the question, *who gives this woman away?* My father died years earlier. The minister was told that I would not say the words *with all my worldly goods, I thee endow*. He agreed not to include it. After all, we were marrying in the eyes of God rather than a civil ritual for the state.

As the minister read the opening of the wedding ceremony, I stared at the pleated, white curtain. A camera peeked through a hole. The red light was off, thank goodness. I didn't want a record of an empty church behind us.

The minister continued, and my thoughts turned back to Richard. He was a good, gentle man, who cared about me and treated me with respect. He valued me and would never raise his hand in anger toward me.

Even though we joked about the I'm-just-a-woman thing, we both knew that when he insisted on having the last word, he would use two: *Yes, dear*. My fears were rooted in leftover values from a long-ago life. They had nothing to do with our present time. Maybe I was a little sad because I was marrying too late for my parents to be here. However, I was ready to share my life with Richard.

When the minister addressed Richard, I felt someone's eyes on my back. Glancing over my shoulder, I noticed the receptionist standing at the rear of the chapel. She was our witness. I didn't know her name. Perhaps I'd be able to read it on the certificate if she had legible handwriting.

The minister asked us to turn and face each other. Richard looked right at me. There was love in his eyes. Or was it appreciation? Or acceptance? Did it even matter, as long as he wanted me?

"Do you, Richard, take Lynn to be your lawfully wedded wife?

Do you promise to—"

"I do." He was still looking straight at me. He would not lie in front of God.

"And do you, Lynn, take this man, Richard, to be your lawfully wedded husband? Do you promise to love, honor, and cherish him as long as you both shall live?"

"I do." I did not promise to obey or let him be the head of the household. We would work that out day by day, issue by issue.

"I now pronounce you husband and wife. You may kiss the bride."

Richard and I smiled at the same time. He put an arm around me and his kiss was warm and moist and tender. The kiss that sealed our marriage felt real and right. We were lawfully married, even though we didn't bother with the legal paperwork, and we were married in a way that fit our needs as well as God's.

Richard turned to the minister and said, "I'm a minister too. I wonder if I could have a copy of your message. I liked what you said." Back to business.

I didn't mean to be cynical. One of the reasons I loved Richard was that he was a skilled multi-tasker.

"I'll check my files and meet you out front," he replied.

If there was recessional music, I didn't remember it. We walked back down the aisle of the empty chapel. This time when Richard kissed me, no one was watching. He had a huge, happy grin plastered across his face.

He believed that marriage was forever. He never changed his mind. I, however, still wasn't fully convinced I should have married him, although I wanted it to last.

"Let me open the door for you, Mrs. Brown."

Though I kept my maiden name, hearing him call me Mrs. Brown felt nice.

I smiled as I replied, "Thank you, Mr. Brown."

* * *

It was after eleven by the time Richard and I were man and wife. How I hated that expression—a throwback to the Fifties. If I thought of it as trying on a role instead of becoming a wife, I felt safer. I could side-step the level of commitment I didn't feel, and get to the physical stuff I knew nothing about, with a close friend whom I trusted.

Richard accepted what I was and what I wasn't, and he still wanted to take me on.

Parked in a darkened alley, I pulled out my laptop and searched for dog-friendly hotels. After a couple of false starts, we found one close by. When Richard called, they had a room. Less than five minutes and five blocks later, we pulled up front.

Mikko and I waited in the car while Richard registered. How much would it hurt? Would I be okay? I would have asked Mikko if I thought he could answer. Then again, what would he know? Not only was he a dog, he was also a male.

Will the pleasure surpass the pain? I wondered as I petted him. What if the pain felt good, like scratching an itch? Everybody did this. My high school students did. It was a part of life, but not for me—not yet.

"It's going to be fine," I said, continuing to run my fingers through Mikko's curly hair. We already figured out the tough things and it was okay. We wanted to be together. And maybe the physical part would be as mysterious and delightful as I heard.

Richard returned and grabbed our bags.

"Let's go," he said with irrepressible enthusiasm and a wide grin. The elevator serenaded us with rickety clanking sounds. "Those gears need greasing. Won't happen before morning."

I almost said that the garage elevator at Kaiser had sounded even worse for years. It was still transporting people from floor to floor. This, however, was not the time to enter into any kind of one-upmanship.

Mikko sniffed at the three doors we passed on the fifth floor. It seemed that we were concentrating a little too hard on finding the right room. Richard dropped the card into the lock. I turned on the lights. It was not elegant. Pet-friendly hotels seldom are. It would do. Besides, we'd only be there for one night.

How would this work? Would Richard be flashing back to his previous honeymoons? Would I be able to give him what he wants?

"You hungry?" he asked.

I nodded and replied, "Are you?"

"There ought to be something in the hotel that's still open."

We found a café, split a sandwich, and it was time. More than time.

"Want to watch a little TV or are you ready for bed?" he asked.

I rolled my eyes, picked up the remote, offered it to him, and said, "Tough one. You decide."

He yawned. "The news is over, and there's probably nothing good on."

"Okay," I nodded like a bobble-head.

He entered the bathroom. I slipped into a nightgown that once belonged to my mother. I hadn't taken time to shop. I usually slept in t-shirts and pajama bottoms and hoped that this would be a bit more alluring. Whatever that meant to Richard.

Pulling down the covers, I sat on the bed, staring at the TV. Probably more as a distraction than anything else. Richard sat next to me and smiled. Taking the remote from my hand, he turned off the TV.

Leaning toward me, he whispered, "I love you."

"I love you too." And I did.

"Nothing to be afraid of, you know," he said, sliding his hand under my nightgown.

His fingertips felt warm, and I willed myself to relax. This could be fun. Many women thought so.

The elevator clanked. Our room was right next to it. Mikko barked.

Richard rolled away and said, "I'm going to put him in the bathroom."

After moving the dog and his water, he returned. "Now, where were we?"

"Were you about to kiss me?"

He did, and we continued exploring. But there was trouble in paradise. After a few minutes he asked, "Would you mind if I went to the adult store that we passed on the way here?"

I wanted to say, *alone? Really? What husband leaves his bride alone on their wedding night?* Maybe a sixty-seven-year-old in need of a little assistance. He could throw on his clothes, leave, and return much more quickly if I stayed behind. After all, we were a team and I was used to being alone.

Before he left, he turned on the TV and handed me the remote. As soon as he was out the door, I turned down the volume. Alone on my honeymoon. No way did I want to pursue that thought. Turning the volume back up, I channel surfed. True to his word, he was back within twenty minutes.

After spilling the contents of the plain brown bag onto the dresser he said, "I'll show you how these work in a couple minutes. First, I need to do one thing." He turned off the lights. When his warm lips covered mine, I shivered expectantly.

* * *

He was already awake the next morning when I opened my eyes.

"You okay?"

"Sure," I said with a flirty feeling in my heart and a smile on my lips.

"How did you sleep?" His irrepressible grin and his eyes told me that he liked what we did.

"Like a baby."

"Ah. Satisfied."

I stretched. Waking up as the wife of a man who would love me and take care of me 'till death do us part, I flashed to an old poster from my college days. Today was the first day of the rest of my life. In this new life, my husband found me attractive and desirable. Act III for him—at least as far as marriage goes. Act I for me. If opening night of my first act was any indication of my new life, then I was going to love being his wife.

CHAPTER 30

THE SUNDAY AFTER our marriage, we were dressing for church when Richard said, "I have a favor to ask."

I stared at him.

"Could you sit up front today?"

Church members often encouraged me to move to the front. So had Richard. I preferred staying in the back. Mostly because I loved observing the congregation. Many of the church members fascinated me. People talked across the aisles before the service, which now seemed normal. They were just being themselves. If they asked a question during the service, it was because they were involved and wanted to know more. In this informal church, we didn't have rituals. God cared about beliefs more than rituals. Of that I was sure.

Even though I didn't play the piano or clean the kitchen, I became a part of his church family. Often, Richard would discuss ideas for messages with me. Sometimes we talked about the church breakfast. Other times, we talked about upcoming events, or gave rides. Many people were between addresses, as Richard liked to say.

Richard was used to living close to the church. People knew that they could call for any emergency. Although I lived thirty-five minutes away, in light traffic, I was not willing to give up my condo. By the time we married, Richard fully understood that. He loved driving and was willing to make the commute to his office and church. Or perhaps he was willing to make the compromise. Once a few of his business associates told him that he was moving up in the world when he gave them his new address, he was happier with the new location. I drove the commute on Sunday mornings, which was easy. On Wednesday nights, I had plenty of time to listen to my books on tape. Sometimes, the commute took over two hours for a one-hour Bible study, which helped me appreciate Richard's commute. I didn't mind.

After a few weeks, I asked why he was the only one reading in Bible study. I thought that it was because he didn't want to put people with reading challenges on the spot. I wanted to open the process up so that everyone could be involved.

Given the opportunity, people did volunteer as I thought they would. Seven months later, almost everyone took turns. Because there were multiple voices and reading styles, people seemed to follow more closely.

Someone would always ask a question that would lead to another, which led to another. Richard never minded going off subject—it was when people learned the most. With his unique experience, as both a student and a businessman, he was an excellent leader for this group.

On Sunday mornings, young children squirmed next to their parents or ran back and forth between the playroom and Mommy's lap. I noticed people changing their seats so they could hear well. When I sat up front, the congregation studied me. I wanted to remain an observer. But now that I was Richard's wife, more would be expected of me. As I stood in front of the mirror at home, I no longer had the option to grin and say, *I'm not your wife.* Sometimes marriage created a shift in power.

In addition, he had an ulterior motive. "I'm going to tell the church that we're married. Will you come up when I ask you to?"

"Sure."

What did he think I was going to do? Refuse? Standing with him was the least I could do. His congregation had not been invited to the service, even though they imagined being a part of it for months. Maybe this was a way of making it up to them.

I once watched a newly married couple take two candles, and together they lit one between them. I loved the symbolism. So did Richard. Should we do that in front of his congregation? They could then be involved in a part of our service. Before I could get the question out, he switched subjects. Oh well. We didn't use candles at his church, and he didn't like it when I said that they could open a portal between this world and the next. So, I let it go.

"Can you help me with my tie?"

I made sure his collar covered the back and decided that changing the subject kept us out of dangerous territory. He was concentrating to ensure that everything was just right for his big announcement. I wouldn't embarrass him.

As always, I picked my battles, and this wasn't one of them. A little compromise goes a long way. He remained nervous on our drive to the church. He didn't need to worry. We were married now. I would cooperate. We didn't need to put on a show for anyone. I already planned to be the kind of wife who would do as my husband asked—whenever I agreed to it.

At the start of Bible study, an hour before church, Richard told everyone sitting around the table, "I have something to announce; however, the big announcement will be in church. Lynn and I went to Reno on Friday and—"

"And you got married?" a tattooed woman at the far end of the table asked, clapping her hands like a child before he could finish his sentence.

"I couldn't say." His trademark answer made me smile. He still used it whenever he didn't want to lie.

They turned to me. I held up my left hand, wearing the same ring as before. "I couldn't say either," I smiled.

It was no surprise to anyone when he asked me to come up front during the service.

"Everyone, this is my wife, Lynn." He practically exploded with pride.

We kissed, while the congregation applauded.

One woman yelled out, "We thought you were getting married when you went to Las Vegas a couple weeks ago."

Another asked, "What do I call you now? Mrs. Pastor?"

"Why don't you keep calling me Lynn?" My face ached from grinning.

More and more people called me Miss Lynn or Mrs. Lynn. I didn't know if that was a Baptist tradition, part of my husband's Texas culture, or simply a sign of respect. I was at least twenty years older than most of the congregation, and maybe it was out of respect for my age.

Richard's previous girlfriend still attended our services. By now, I knew her fairly well. If he was running late, he called and asked me to pick her up. She didn't drive.

She wasn't in church the day Richard announced our marriage. She received the news by phone, after church, and she heard it from me. I called all the women about an upcoming conference, starting each conversation with, "Hi, this is Lynn Goodwin . . . Goodwin-Brown." If the addition on my last name registered, she never acknowledged it.

Instead, she said that she couldn't attend. That was normal. Every year she stayed home with her cat, who received four heart pills evenly spaced throughout the day.

Hanging up, I told Richard about our conversation.

"I don't think she understood. Can I borrow your phone to call her back?" After punching in the number, I handed it to him. "I wanted to be sure you heard that Lynn and I were married over the weekend."

"I know," I think she said, though her voice was garbled.

Told you so, I thought, looking straight at him. It was one more piece of proof that I was competent, and he did not have to take care of me.

A year earlier, when he broke off his relationship with the woman, he warned her, "You'll miss me when I'm gone."

She never seemed to miss him. Either that or she was numb. Over and over during our rides to church she insisted she was happy that we found each other. She said loved him, but wasn't in love with him.

By now, the line between love and being in love was growing faint. Richard and I ate out together, watched movies together, and often went away for the weekend. He was a good sounding board, even though he didn't know any more about writing than I did about electricity. His ideas often stimulated new thoughts or sent me off in a different direction. Surely, I was growing to love him more each day.

More often than not, I was amused rather than annoyed by his instructions. He explained how to buy groceries, how to bake a potato or slice a piece of meat, how to drive a car, and he sometimes tried to tell me how to think. His suggestions usually bounced off me like a rubber ball thrown against a cement wall.

He still wanted to do things for me. Always claiming that I was the weaker sex. Hah! If he saw me as weak, then he wasn't seeing all of me unless he was talking about my physical strength. In that category, I was definitely the weaker one.

He asked for spelling help so often that I started answering the phone with "Goodwin-Brown Spelling Service." I read more than he did, although he had a fabulous retention of audio books. In restaurants, I noticed the ambiance and the cleanliness. He noticed the light fixtures. Though I proved I was a competent driver, he still cringed and corrected me from the passenger seat. More and more, however, he closed his eyes for a quick nap.

He once said, "You shouldn't have to drive in rush-hour traffic." Then added, "I guess you've been doing it all of your life."

His generalizations about women didn't work for me. As long as he realized that, this marriage just might last.

CHAPTER 31

THAT SUMMER, WE lost our little Mikko. Mikko loved me enough to make room for Richard. Did my little companion instinctually know I would outlive him and want me to have someone in my life? Of course, I was giving a dog too much credit. However, they sometimes sensed that their purpose was to protect the people who cared for them. Now I understood why Mikko didn't bark the first time Richard came to the door. His trust meant something.

Three weeks after his death, we adopted Mikko's honorary younger brother. Eddie, a sixteen-pound terrier, needed a home because his owner was moving to Utah. Although Mikko and Eddie had the same black-and-white coloring, they were very different breeds, sort of like Richard and me. Eddie was more open, energetic, and fun-loving than Mikko, who had a stubborn, independent streak a mile wide.

Richard wanted to help pick out our new dog. Until he met Eddie. Who could resist the way he rolled over and showed us his tummy, asking to be petted and scratched? Eddie was full of life and energy. Our new furry son needed us, and we loved coming home to him.

To his credit, Richard never complained about my laundry methods or my vacuuming habits or my casual approach to housekeeping. I left stacks of books and papers on the coffee table, the trunk, the drum table in our living room, the desk in our bedroom, and the floor of my office. Most of the books had been sent to me for review. He never complained. He had his own stacks on his desk. Since we were not raising children, neatness didn't matter to us.

Although he was happy to let me pursue my interests, Richard sometimes wanted more time with me than I could give—especially if I had a deadline. Certainly he'd help out more if I asked him to. Housework just wasn't his thing. Maybe someday we would clean the kitchen cupboards or the garage together. Maybe not. Our priorities lay elsewhere.

The condo that I guarded so closely had become *our* place, even though his name wasn't on the deed. It became second nature to share what used to be my space, my car, and my life. I didn't let go of my control. I just exchanged parts of it for something better.

Most of our domestic challenges were still in the kitchen. My skills suited me. However, Richard didn't think pushing buttons on a microwave was cooking. He let me wash dishes, clean the stove, and sometimes he tried to teach me how to slice and chop to his standards. How did he think I cooked before we met? What message did he receive when I refused to deep-fry food or pour salt all over it? My best compromise was to buy a saltshaker with bigger holes for the table. Laughably, he bought one with even bigger holes for the stove.

Richard cooked when his kids were growing up, and he missed it. He believed that the kitchen was the center of the house. Mine was more like a postage stamp—the kind you find in a first apartment. I shook it off. With my weight issues, I didn't need the kitchen to be the center of anything. He didn't like the size of my kitchen any more than I liked the size of his saltshaker.

Without complaint, I did the laundry, and Richard never criticized my cold cycles or how I folded. He even ignored his work shirts and jeans sitting in the washing machine for several days before I ran it. Shopping was my responsibility, paying for his brand of coffee, his vitamins, and his razor blades. Apparently, this was what a traditional housewife did, especially if she didn't work outside the home. I actually told him that once and he agreed. Though, he added, that a husband should give his wife money for her purchases. Hello, 1950s.

Richard had no experience as a liberated husband. Not long after my initial surprise, I let go of my resentments around doing his personal shopping. I simply wasn't used to spending my money on someone else. I gave to charities. I was a wife and sometimes I was afraid that he thought that *wife* was a synonym for servant. No wonder God put us together. We both had so much to learn.

I wanted to be married. However, battles or power struggles I could do without.

When Richard taught me about buying and selling cars, he said that everything had its price. Therefore, why not walk up to a total stranger and ask if the car was for sale? His stories about being a father to seven children explained why he had no room for loneliness in his life. He was completely unfamiliar with the concept. He believed that marriage was forever, which made me feel secure.

Together, we found compromises. More and more, Richard and I ate out. Oddly, we shared meals in a restaurant even though our tastes hadn't changed. Richard ordered, while taking my likes and dislikes into account. No problem. I could always snack later if I absolutely hated the meal. I was happy to hand him a twenty before walking into Mel's or Outback. Sharing the check somehow made me feel equal.

One night I prepared a beefsteak tomato stuffed with tuna salad and garnished with avocado slices. Richard offered to bring a packaged salad, even though this was a tuna and tomato salad. I said no. Clearly he didn't understand but he agreed.

As I prepared the salad, I discovered that the tomatoes weren't quite ripe and the avocado was a little mushy. Richard didn't complain. I left an onion with the salt and pepper beside his portion. He approved.

He even said, "You were right. This is enough food."

About half way through the meal, I asked, "You've been very nice about this meal. What would you do differently?"

He stared at me, started to say something, shook his head, and replied, "Nothing."

"It's okay. I'm asking." At that moment, he could say what he wanted and I wouldn't feel like he was ramming it down my throat. "I know the tomatoes and the avocado aren't quite right. One's too ripe and the other's not ripe enough. Are you supposed to smell tomatoes?" My sense of smell didn't work.

"I've never smelled a tomato."

"But . . ."

"Okay. As long as you asked, the onion was wrong."

I let out a breath I hadn't realized I was holding. "I got the sweet yellow ones. The sign said so."

"It was bitter. And the sign didn't say that's what it was." How did he know what the sign on the bin said? He wasn't even there.

"But . . ."

"I threw it away," he said. "It's fine like this."

"What else?"

"It's okay," he replied.

"Please tell me."

When did he become afraid to let me know what he thought? We were both working so hard at not offending one another that we were avoiding the truth. Was there a deeper problem, and did it have anything to do with food?

"If I were doing it, I'd cut the celery thinner."

"Okay. I can do that."

This was one more discrepancy between the way I'd been taught and the way he liked his food. I never told him that. Slicing celery thinner couldn't be that hard, as long as I didn't slice my finger by mistake.

"This is really good. It's something different," he said.

I loved him for that because he was trying to please me.

"Would you like ice cream for dessert?" I asked.

He grinned, and I was glad I offered the right thing.

"Will you dish it?" I asked. He was always proud to help out.

By the time I loaded the dishwasher, Richard was on the phone with a client. Walking Eddie through the park, I stated, "I'm still not sure what's going on between us. It's silly to have such a power struggle."

Eddie wagged and sniffed.

CHAPTER 32

IN JUNE, WE traveled as husband and wife. Running a workshop at the Story Circle Network Conference in Austin excited me. Richard dropped me off on his way to Needville to see his family. Walking into the hotel with a ring on my finger and a relationship in my heart, I beamed with happiness. This weekend gave me the opportunity to spend time with women who came to network, learn, and explore new ways of telling their stories. How would the single and divorced women feel about my enthusiasm for my new marriage? Would anyone notice the ring guard?

During the convention, I rediscovered the power of my experience. If I wrote about Richard and me, the story would be more original than one of me caring for my mother. Those types of stories had been written many times. But how often did a widower seeking his third wife find a woman who's never been married in the Craigslist ads? The looks of fascination and amazement from people when I talked about a memoir seemed promising.

"I'd buy that," said one woman after another.

After the first meeting ended, I went to my room. The blinking red phone light meant that I had a message. Juliana, a woman I coached online, wanted to meet for dinner. She was a math teacher with a published book of poetry and strong confidence. She lived a couple of hours away and came to the conference alone. Just as I used to do.

It was a pleasure to have dinner with such a decisive and determined woman. Especially one who wrote appreciatively about the land that surrounded her. She spoke with an edge of attitude about the people who didn't understand the importance of nature. She reminded me of myself before I met Richard. Like so many women at the conference, Julianna was divorced. I never did hear the full story. Figured she'd tell me in a heartbeat if she wanted me to know. Moving her writing career forward at her own pace was just one sign that she was taking responsibility for herself. Delighted to hear about Richard and me, her laughter filled the room when I said I found him on Craigslist. Much as I didn't want to care what she thought, I basked in her approval.

I carried that approval with me the next morning as I walked into the Heart-to-Heart Coaching Sessions. Dressed in a loose green sweater I had owned for at least twenty-five years, I smiled. Adding the pearls my hubby gave me for Christmas, I resembled a professional coach.

Just before the first session started, a woman with soft, graying curls sat down in front of me.

"Hello," she whispered.

"I'm sorry?" I couldn't hear her with all the chatter around us.

Leaning across the table she said, "How do I start my story?"

"What's it about?"

She could barely explain her confusion over a personal situation that changed her life. She reminded me of those I tutored in the adult literacy program. Although they had great stories to tell, they didn't know how to start. Unlike them, she knew how to write. She was just overwhelmed by the possibilities and her lack of focus.

"Why don't you pick an active scene that will set some stakes and give roots to your characters? Make us care what happens to them. Start fairly far into the story."

She wrote down what I said. Amazing. My high school students rarely wrote down anything. I loved working with people who wanted my help.

The next woman that plopped down read a brief synopsis from a folded sheet of paper. "Do you think this will sell?"

I leaned in. The noise was worse than a rock concert.

"I won't know until you get your whole story on paper. Your idea is a good one."

"Does punctuation really matter?" a third woman asked.

Stretching out my back, I replied, "You can get an editor to help with that when you're ready."

"Where would I find an editor?"

I handed her a card. "If I'm not the right person, Google 'editors for memoirs.' Ask questions before you sign a contract."

The next author stared at the tablecloth. "Who'd be interested about a farm in Texas?"

I waited for her to look up before answering. "Anyone who hasn't lived that life. Why do you want to tell your story?"

These women had experiences that someone else said they should share. They wanted to write about the frustration that came from doing laundry and dishes and transporting kids, year after year. Others were ready to admit that they allowed themselves to live like second-class citizens. Deceiving themselves by calling it love. Not realizing that the details and the circumstances might take care of it, many were uncertain how to make their stories unique. They didn't want to trivialize what they'd been through.

Listening to their fears encouraged me to look at my own and share my story. I gave up sixty-two years of independence for a marriage. I believe that I'm better off married, most of the time.

I twisted the ring on my finger as we walked to our next session.

The ring guard scraped my skin. I now had companionship and the private joys of a partner. My anxiety remained low while my gratitude soared.

CHAPTER 33

THE VALIDATION I received from the women at the SCN conference opened me up. The women reinforced the worth of my techniques, which boosted my self-worth as much as Richard's amazement and praise. For the first time, I felt empowered as a writer, a teacher, and a wife.

Richard and I attended the closing luncheon together. I explained that a professional who taught about writing memoirs and a writer working on her third memoir were at the table. By the time the meal was over, Richard saw me in a different light. He came away saying, "They really respect you."

After lunch, Richard carried my suitcase to the car. As we drove away, it felt good to be a married writer. The perspective of other people and the three days apart made us seem somehow closer to each other. So did seeing him interacting with my peers. I had stories to tell, and the people at the conference said that they couldn't wait until my memoir hit the bookstores. What a stimulating experience.

That summer, I worked on teaching classes, selling my published book, and finding a publisher for my coming of age novel,

TALENT—a novel filled with teen drama, heartbreak, hope, and issues relevant to teens and their families. Plus, it had potential for a sequel. As novels arrived for review, my days filled with more work than I could ever finish in a lifetime. I embraced it. Richard and I both loved being busy.

Richard concentrated on writing proposals for electrical jobs, submitting bids, and meeting payroll. On Saturday nights and Sunday mornings, he concentrated on his message for the church, often waking up at five in the morning to finish up before waking me at seven-thirty to type up his sermon. He was giving me space to live my life and, at the same time, filling me with a new understanding of what really mattered.

On a crisp September Sunday afternoon, we were enjoying our drive out of the Sierras, until our phones beeped simultaneously. We must have been back in range of the cell towers.

Two of his adult children, Sam and Sarah, both needed to talk to their father. They'd left messages on my phone when they couldn't reach his. My stomach fluttered. Last Thanksgiving, Sam lost his front teeth playing football. What was it this time?

We each reached for our phones.

"Call your older sister!" Sam ordered his dad at the same time Sarah asked, "Can you have Dad call Aunt Marsha as soon as possible?"

I searched for her listing so Richard could talk on his blue tooth as he maneuvered the truck and trailer down a curvy mountain road.

"I'm sorry," he said almost immediately. "When did it happen?"

Though I could only hear his side of the conversation, I knew what Marsha had said. I could hear it in the tone of Richard's voice. His father's health had been declining for some time. That morning, he passed away. My stomach churned. What did you say to your spouse when he just lost a parent?

"I'm so sorry," I said as soon as the call ended.

I hated the cliché, but what else was there to say? Never at a loss for words, Richard shared the details of the call with me as he continued to maneuver the two-lane road shadowed by dense pine branches. The timing must have shocked me more than him. I guess he'd been expecting it for months.

Assuming he had more calls to make, I asked, "Want me to drive?" I wanted to help, even if it just gave him the opportunity to notify his kids that their grandfather was gone.

"No. I'm fine."

He called Sarah, who offered to purchase the plane tickets for everyone in the family.

"She can put ours on our Southwest card," I whispered across the console. That was code for *I'll pay the bill.* Some of the companies he worked for were slow to pay, and I wasn't about to let a lack of cash keep him from his own father's funeral. It was the right thing to do. As soon as he finished the call he thanked me.

We met up with two of Richard's daughters, Beth and Sarah, at the Oakland Airport and flew to Houston Hobby together. The daughters had arranged their own transportation in Texas, so Richard and I rented a car. We drove alone to Corpus Christi, without the rest of the family. Since he drove me through his old neighborhood on an earlier trip, we headed straight to the hotel. The same hotel where his brother and sisters were staying. After conversation and a dinner, we went to our room.

While we were getting ready for the funeral, Richard asked if I'd iron his black shirt. Normally, I never ironed. "Can you make an exception to your rule of no ironing this one time?"

I searched for the iron but found its surface was old and rusty. Shaking the shirt over and over, I said, "It's black. No one will see the wrinkles."

At the cemetery, a white canopy next to the grassy place where his mother was buried caught our attention. Richard walked on ahead with his funeral book in hand. I made my way across the grass after talking with one of his grandkids, watching for unevenness in the lawn. The last thing I wanted to do was trip and fall. Wanting to hide out in the back, I froze when Richard asked, "Where have you been?"

"I was—"

"Your seat is right there. People are waiting." He pointed to a seat at the end of the front row, next to his brother and sisters. I saw myself as an outsider. Clearly, he did not.

After a prayer and a bit of scripture, Richard invited everyone to stand and share their memories. I'd been lucky enough to meet his father. When his kids and grandkids told their stories about the man, I enjoyed imagining his face and hearing his voice. Beth's description of his grilled cheese sandwiches really stood out in my mind. Later, Richard told me that he, too, could make them. They were fried, not deep-fried. I'd be proud to eat a Brown-family sandwich.

Hearing one grandchild after another talk about the lamp or the dresser or the mirror that Grandpa had crafted for them, I was impressed by his outreach. Bill had been a skilled woodworker as well as an inventive electrician. He triggered his son's interest in the craft.

Jena was going to sign a song, although no one in the family had hearing problems, but had technical difficulties with her computer. I pushed a few buttons, and the sound came to life. As I sat down again, it occurred to me that I was sitting up front for Richard. Just as I sat in the front at his church when he preached. Today wasn't about me. Not at all. I was there as Richard's support system. My presence mattered to him and to his family.

This service was about honoring a patriarch who left this world. Being the oldest son, Richard was now the head of the family. An unexpected status came with being his wife. Didn't matter whether I was with his family, his congregation, or his workers. Thinking about it, I was proud to rise to the occasion.

Though I used to believe that I was more independent without a man, my perceptions changed. Life was about more than doing whatever I wanted. The Browns accepted me exactly as I was, and they cared what happened to both Richard and me. I didn't realize, until that day, how badly I craved this level of acceptance. It was nice to have an unconditionally supportive family.

After the service, the whole extended family drove to a nearby Mexican restaurant. Sitting at a long table that filled most of the room, I listened while everyone talked, catching up on each other's lives. When they asked me about my life, I explained that I was a writer, a writing coach, an editor, and a new wife.

After lunch, we gathered in front of the restaurant, and Marsha, an award-winning photographer, snapped pictures. Every branch of the family and every combination of people were present. It was spirited and semi-chaotic, like all of the Brown gatherings. Everyone talked at the same time. No one was bothered by all the noise or worried about what they might be missing.

Before everyone left, Richard's brother and sisters gathered in our motel room to talk about Bill's estate. Though I offered to leave, Richard asked me to stay. Marsha's spouse was there, too. She was the oldest, a retired math teacher, and the executor of the will. Bill never made a distinction between his biological children and his wife's children from her first marriage. He would have given Marsha and Richard his last name, but the family decided that Dick Brown's children should keep his name to keep the memory of their biological father alive. It was the least they could do for a Navy pilot who was shot down over Saipan. Bill Huffman was the only father Richard ever knew. Bill was, in all respects, Richard's dad.

Most of his money had already been spent on round-the-clock caregivers. What was left was to be divided equally among the four of them. The rest of the inheritance was property in Indiana, where they each held equal shares. As they talked, I learned about the issues around access and right-of-ways. Would we make a trip to Indiana to look at it? Before I could ask, Richard gave his share to his brother. It simplified matters. We already received his parent's Thousand Trails membership a few months earlier and were enjoying the campgrounds whenever we could get away.

Although the loss was sad, there was a small joy for me. Everyone accepted and welcomed me as Richard's new wife. I'd never been a mother, so I became friends with Richard's adult children. Hearing his grandchildren call me Grandma Lynn sent ripples of pride and joy through my heart. I hadn't lost my old life after all. Instead, I made it bigger than ever.

CHAPTER 34

A COUPLE MONTHS after the conference, I received the Story Circle Network newsletter. Pictures from the workshops were included. I looked for the photos of me leading participants through a physicality exercise, in which writers tried on their character's bodies and attitudes. Not there. Instead, I found a picture of Richard and me together, his arm around me. I remembered the photographer saying, "I want to capture the newlyweds," as she snapped our picture. Once again, I saw the joy on my face. This time, I thought of Cinderella more than Yosemite. Richard and I were a fairy tale for seniors.

Young people have weddings and celebrations with white dresses and flowers. Richard and I have maturity and a relationship built on trust and love and needs that I never realized I had. Sometimes I think of that statement from the Vassar catalogue I read before my freshman year: *If you are one of the 93% who eventually marry . . .*

When I first read that statement, I was eighteen and had only been on two dates. The phrase—*eventually marry*—gave me hope. Forty-four years later, I was finally ready to share my life. And, perhaps, lucky enough to find the right man. My first instincts about Richard were correct. If we didn't care that we met on Craigslist, why should anyone else?

* * *

A few weeks after his dad's funeral, Richard called from his office. Marsha had sent him his share of the estate.

The first thing he did was pay back the loans I made to his business. When he called to give me the news, I considered forgiving the whole amount.

"Don't even mention it unless you really mean it," Richard told me.

I said no more. He was prepared to do the honorable thing, and I let him. For one thing, I didn't want to risk making a choice I would later regret.

One night, shortly after I deposited his check, we were seated in a nearly empty coffee shop, waiting for the steak and potato we would share for dinner. Richard leaned across the table and took my hand in his. Instead of saying grace, as we normally did, he asked, "How would you like a ring of your own?"

Unbelievable as it seemed, my first instinct was to say, *oh no, I love this ring*. The fact that such a statement even flashed through my head startled me. I hadn't realized I accepted it as mine—ring guard and all. The shift happened so gradually that I didn't even notice. I now loved wearing Joan's ring even though I wanted my own. However, I already accepted that it would probably never happen. Thank goodness he hadn't forgotten his promise to get me one when he could. The ring would be a physical manifestation of our unique love, as it was for every married couple.

I stared at the rose gold ring with the diamonds sparkling on the edges. The ring with the visible sizer.

"That would be nice," I replied in a voice that sounded more serene than I felt.

Months earlier, I bought him a gold ring with eight tiny diamonds to replace the titanium one we picked out in Reno. He wore it all the time. It was sturdy, attractive, and good looking. When we were selecting it, I asked him to be sure it was strong enough so that he couldn't possibly hurt it. Of course, I would have forgiven him if anything happened. I just wanted him to be comfortable with an all-occasion ring. Because the diamonds were flush with the surface, they would never fall out. To him, it was exactly right.

Standing at the jewelry counter to pick out my own ring, I felt appreciated and valued. My old fears suddenly seemed small and silly. We gazed at the wedding rings, resting beneath the glass in their elegant settings, until an eager young woman hurried over to help us. She pulled out one case at a time. With each ring, Richard asked if I liked it.

As we were bantering about the choices, the clerk asked, "How long have you two been married?"

"Forty-six years," Richard answered. "This is my third wife."

She looked from him to me, and I said, "About seven months. He's giving you a cumulative total."

"It's her first marriage," Richard added with the grin that I loved.

"It's never too late," I said, thinking of the car metaphor that first attracted me to him.

We picked out the ring that I wear today. The clerk sent it off to be sized. It would be on my finger within a week. I walked out of the store with my husby holding my hand. The night was cool, and my heart was warm. The sky was filled with the same stars I admired on our first date. They twinkled over us as if the whole universe were giving its approval.

NOTE FROM THE AUTHOR—RESOURCES

IT'S BEEN FIVE years since we were married. Richard and I are still together and happy. He says, "The secret to marriage is no secrets." I say, "Pick your battles," and I almost always add, "and this isn't one of them." Here are a few resources to help you find Mr. Right or Ms. Open-and-Happy.

Online Dating

I had some bad luck before I met Richard, and I haven't tried most of these commercial sites. But what's the harm in looking? Go online; however, bring along your common sense. Put your fears on a back burner, but don't take them off the stove. Maybe one of these sites will change your life. Craigslist changed mine. Truthfully, though, I changed my own life. Site owners did not pay to be listed here and this is not a comprehensive list.

1. http://www.itsjustlunch.com/
2. http://ourtime.com
3. http://craigslist.com
4. http://eharmony.com
5. www.50plus-club.com/Dating

None of these interest you? No problem. Maybe you'll find the perfect ad later. Since I found a one-in-a-million man on Craigslist, he's no longer available.

Try Another Strategy

Join a group that shares your interests:

1. Book club?
2. Golfing lessons?
3. Film group?
4. Computer club?
5. Co-ed poker?
6. Cooking class?
7. Baseball team?
8. Church?
9. Meetups for seniors?
10. Google "Social Groups for Seniors Near Me"

Articles and a Video to Help You Find the Right Partner

(especially if you're over fifty)

1. Today Show interview with AARP expert Pepper Schwartz, PhD: https://www.today.com/video/small-but-smart-exercise-moves-for-each-day-of-the-week-1035064899939

2. A bit of self-help from Lisa Copeland: http://www.huffingtonpost.com/lisa-copeland/dating-after-50_b_9873706.html
3. Some realism: https://www.zoosk.com/date-mix/over-50-dating/what-men-over-50-want/
4. Relationships for grandparents: http://www.grandparents.com/family-and-relationships/dating-and-marriage-and-sex/how-to-date
5. Figure it out for yourself with these sentence starts: http://www.huffingtonpost.com/lisa-copeland/law-of-attraction_b_12377914.html

Don't spend too much time online, though. The man or woman of your dreams is somewhere out in the world.

So, what do you do? Go to coffee with your buddies. Meet friends for lunch. Volunteer. A million places could use your help. You'll open up a whole new world, and one strategy will lead to another.

Want to share your story of finding a great mate when you're over 50? Send it to Lgood67334@comcast.net. We are likely to post it on Facebook or at blynngoodwin.com if we have your permission to do so.

Remember, there are no mistakes, only new material. Have fun exploring the pros and cons of potential relationships. It will make you a happier person.

ACKNOWLEDGEMENTS

Miracles happen. My relationship with Richard and this book are two examples.

I want to thank all the women at the Story Circle Network Conference in 2012 and the IWWG Summer Conferences in 2014 and 2015 who validated my story. Thanks to the free writing group I've been with since 2003, who encouraged me to tell all in my unique voice.

Thank you to face-to-face teachers Joan Marie Wood, Andy Couturier, Joyce Maynard, and online teachers Wendy Dale and Waverley Fitzgerald. All of you added depth and perspective at different times in the process.

I appreciate those who listened to me read early portions out loud. Your questions always made me dig deeper. Kathy Briccetti, Veronica Chater, Suzanne LaFetra Collier, Annie Kassof, Sybil Lockhart, and Rachel Sarah thank you for encouraging me to write about my awakening sexuality, whether I used what I wrote or not. You increased my courage.

Thanks also to the regular members of my Shush and Write Group; Jill Hedgecock, Aline Soules, and Ann Steiner, PhD. Our week-to-week check ins helped me stay on track.

Special thanks to John Koehler and Joe Coccaro, owners of Koehler Press and my excellent editor there, Lynn Moon, and my proofreader, Hannah Woodlan.

Thanks also to Larry Carlat, who accepted my very short story about finding my husband at 62 and published it in *Purple Clover.*

CPSIA information can be obtained
at www.ICGtesting.com
Printed in the USA
FSHW010239270919
62398FS